FOREWORD

The collection of "Everything Will Be Okay" travel phrasebooks published by T&P Books is designed for people traveling abroad for tourism and business. The phrasebooks contain what matters most - the essentials for basic communication. This is an indispensable set of phrases to "survive" while abroad.

This phrasebook will help you in most cases where you need to ask something, get directions, find out how much something costs, etc. It can also resolve difficult communication situations where gestures just won't help.

This book contains a lot of phrases that have been grouped according to the most relevant topics. You'll also find a mini dictionary with useful words - numbers, time, calendar, colors...

Take "Everything Will Be Okay" phrasebook with you on the road and you'll have an irreplaceable traveling companion who will help you find your way out of any situation and teach you to not fear speaking with foreigners.

TABLE OF CONTENTS

T&P Books Publishing

Travel phrasebooks collection
«Everything Will Be Okay!»

T&P Books Publishing

PHRASEBOOK
PORTUGUESE

By Andrey Taranov

THE MOST IMPORTANT PHRASES

This phrasebook contains
the most important
phrases and questions
for basic communication
Everything you need
to survive overseas

T&P BOOKS

Phrasebook + 250-word dictionary

English-Portuguese phrasebook & mini dictionary

By Andrey Taranov

The collection of "Everything Will Be Okay" travel phrasebooks published by T&P Books is designed for people traveling abroad for tourism and business. The phrasebooks contain what matters most - the essentials for basic communication. This is an indispensable set of phrases to "survive" while abroad.

You'll also find a mini dictionary with 250 useful words required for everyday communication - the names of months and days of the week, measurements, family members, and more.

T&P Books Publishing
www.tpbooks.com

ISBN: 978-1-78492-408-9

This book is also available in E-book formats.
Please visit www.tpbooks.com or the major online bookstores.

PRONUNCIATION

Letter	Portuguese example	T&P phonetic alphabet	English example
a	patinadora	[a]	shorter than in ask
ã	capitão	[õ]	nasal [a]
b	cabriolé	[b]	baby, book
b [1]	acabar	[β]	between b and v
c [2]	contador	[k]	clock, kiss
c [3]	injector	[s]	silent [s]
c [4]	ambulância	[s]	city, boss
ç	comemoração	[s]	city, boss
ch	champanha	[ʃ]	machine, shark
d	diário	[d]	day, doctor
e	expressão	[ɛ], [ɛː]	habit, bad
e	grau científico	[e]	elm, medal
e	nove	[ə]	driver, teacher
f	fonética	[f]	face, food
g [5]	língua	[g]	game, gold
g [6]	estrangeiro	[ʒ]	forge, pleasure
gu [7]	fogueiro	[g]	game, gold
h [8]	hélice	[h]	silent [h]
i [9]	bandeira	[i]	shorter than in feet
i [10]	sino	[i]	shorter than in feet
j	juntos	[ʒ]	forge, pleasure
k [11]	empresa-broker	[k]	clock, kiss
l	bolsa	[l]	lace, people
lh	escolher	[ʎ]	daily, million
m [12]	menu	[m]	magic, milk
m [13]	passagem	[ŋ]	English, ring
n	piscina	[n]	name, normal
nh	desenho	[ɲ]	canyon, new
o [14]	escola de negócios	[o], [ɔ]	drop, baught
o [15]	ciclismo	[u]	book
p	prato	[p]	pencil, private
qu [16]	qualidade da imagem	[kv]	square, quality
qu [17]	querosene	[k]	clock, kiss
r	forno	[r]	rice, radio
r	resto	[ʁ]	fricative r
s [18]	sereia	[s]	city, boss
ss	passado	[s]	city, boss

Letter	Portuguese example	T&P phonetic alphabet	English example
s [19]	explosivo	[z]	zebra, please
s [20]	rede de lojas	[ʃ]	machine, shark
t	tordo	[t]	tourist, trip
u	truta	[u]	book
v	voar	[v]	very, river
v [21]	savana	[β]	between b and v
w [22]	cow-boy	[u]	book
x [23]	bruxa	[ʃ]	machine, shark
x [24]	exercício	[gz]	exam, exact
y	display	[j]	yes, New York
z [25]	amizade	[z]	zebra, please
z [26]	giz	[ʃ]	machine, shark

Combinations of letters

ia	embraiagem	[ja]	Kenya, piano
io [27]	estado-maior	[jɔ]	New York
io [28]	arroio	[ju]	youth, usually
io [29]	aniversário	[ju]	youth, usually
iu	ciumento	[ju]	youth, usually
un, um	fungo, algum	[ʊn]	soon
in, im	cinco, sim	[ĩ]	meeting, evening
en, em	cento, sempre	[ẽ]	nasal [e]

Comments

[1] usually between vowels
[2] before a, o, u and consonants
[3] before b, d, p, t
[4] in front of e, i
[5] before a, o, u and consonants
[6] before e, i
[7] before e, i
[8] at the beginning of words
[9] unstressed between vowel and consonant
[10] elsewhere
[11] in loanwords only
[12] before vowels and b, p
[13] before consonants and in em, im
[14] stressed
[15] unstressed, before a, e and in do, dos, o, os)
[16] before a, o and ü
[17] before e and i
[18] at the beginning of a word

[19] between vowels
[20] at the end of a word
[21] usually between vowels
[22] in loanwords only
[23] between vowels
[24] in ex- before a vowel
[25] between vowels
[26] at the end of a word
[27] stressed, after vowels
[28] unstressed, after vowels
[29] unstressed, after consonants

LIST OF ABBREVIATIONS

English abbreviations

ab.	-	about
adj	-	adjective
adv	-	adverb
anim.	-	animate
as adj	-	attributive noun used as adjective
e.g.	-	for example
etc.	-	et cetera
fam.	-	familiar
fem.	-	feminine
form.	-	formal
inanim.	-	inanimate
masc.	-	masculine
math	-	mathematics
mil.	-	military
n	-	noun
pl	-	plural
pron.	-	pronoun
sb	-	somebody
sing.	-	singular
sth	-	something
v aux	-	auxiliary verb
vi	-	intransitive verb
vi, vt	-	intransitive, transitive verb
vt	-	transitive verb

Portuguese abbreviations

f	-	feminine noun
f pl	-	feminine plural
m	-	masculine noun
m pl	-	masculine plural
m, f	-	masculine, feminine
pl	-	plural
v aux	-	auxiliary verb

vi	-	intransitive verb
vi, vt	-	intransitive, transitive verb
vp	-	pronominal verb
vt	-	transitive verb

PORTUGUESE PHRASEBOOK

This section contains
important phrases that may
come in handy in various
real-life situations.
The phrasebook will help
you ask for directions, clarify
a price, buy tickets, and
order food at a restaurant

T&P Books Publishing

PHRASEBOOK
CONTENTS

T&P Books Publishing

Excuse me, ...

Desculpe, ...
[dɛʃk'ulpɛ, ...]

Hello.

Olá!
[ɔl'a!]

Thank you.

Obrigado /Obrigada/.
[ɔbrig'adu /ɔbrig'ada/]

Good bye.

Adeus.
[ad'euʃ]

Yes.

Sim.
[sĩ]

No.

Não.
['nau]

I don't know.

Não sei.
['nau sɛj]

Where? | Where to? | When?

Onde? | Para onde? | Quando?
['õdɛ? | 'para 'õdɛ? | ku'ãdu?]

I need ...

Preciso de ...
[prɛs'izu dɛ ...]

I want ...

Eu queria ...
['eu kɛr'ia ...]

Do you have ...?

Tem ...?
[tɛj ...?]

Is there a ... here?

Há aqui ...?
['a ak'i ...?]

May I ...?

Posso ...?
['pɔsu ...?]

..., please (polite request)

..., por favor
[..., pur fav'or]

I'm looking for ...

Estou à procura de ...
[ʃto a prɔk'ura dɛ ...]

restroom

casa de banho
['kaza dɛ 'baɲu]

ATM

Multibanco
[multib'ãku]

pharmacy (drugstore)

farmácia
[farm'asia]

hospital

hospital
[ɔʃpit'al]

police station

esquadra de polícia
[ɛʃku'adra dɛ pul'isia]

subway

metro
['mɛtru]

---

taxi	**táxi** ['taksi]
train station	**estação de comboio** [ɛʃtas'au dɛ kõb'ɔju]

My name is …	**Chamo-me …** ['ʃamumɛ …]
What's your name?	**Como se chama?** ['komu sɛ ʃ'ama?]
Could you please help me?	**Pode-me dar uma ajuda?** ['pɔdɛmɛ dar 'uma aʒ'uda?]
I've got a problem.	**Tenho um problema.** ['tɛɲu ũ prubl'ema]
I don't feel well.	**Não me sinto bem.** ['nau mɛ 'sĩtu bɛj]
Call an ambulance!	**Chame a ambulância!** ['ʃamɛ a ãbul'ãsia!]
May I make a call?	**Posso fazer uma chamada?** ['pɔsu faz'er 'uma ʃam'ada?]

I'm sorry.	**Desculpe.** [dɛʃk'ulpɛ]
You're welcome.	**De nada.** [dɛ 'nada]

I, me	**eu** ['eu]
you (inform.)	**tu** [tu]
he	**ele** ['ɛlɛ]
she	**ela** ['ɛla]
they (masc.)	**eles** ['ɛleʃ]
they (fem.)	**elas** ['ɛlaʃ]
we	**nós** [nɔʃ]
you (pl)	**vocês** [vɔs'eʃ]
you (sg, form.)	**você** [vɔs'e]

ENTRANCE	**ENTRADA** [ẽtr'ada]
EXIT	**SAÍDA** [sa'ida]
OUT OF ORDER	**FORA DE SERVIÇO** [f'ora dɛ sɛrv'isu]
CLOSED	**FECHADO** [fɛʃ'adu]

OPEN	**ABERTO** [ab'ɛrtu]
FOR WOMEN	**PARA SENHORAS** ['para sɛɲ'oraʃ]
FOR MEN	**PARA HOMENS** ['para 'ɔmɛjʃ]

Questions

Where? | **Onde?**
['õdɛ?]

Where to? | **Para onde?**
['para 'õdɛ?]

Where from? | **De onde?**
[dɛ 'õdɛ?]

Why? | **Porquê?**
[purk'e?]

For what reason? | **Porque razão?**
['purkɛ raz'au?]

When? | **Quando?**
[ku'ãdu?]

How long? | **Quanto tempo?**
[ku'ãtu 'tẽpu?]

At what time? | **A que horas?**
[a kɛ 'ɔraʃ?]

How much? | **Quanto?**
[ku'ãtu?]

Do you have ...? | **Tem ...?**
[tɛj ...?]

Where is ...? | **Onde fica ...?**
['õdɛ 'fika ...?]

What time is it? | **Que horas são?**
[kɛ 'ɔraʃ 'sau?]

May I make a call? | **Posso fazer uma chamada?**
['pɔsu faz'er 'uma ʃam'ada?]

Who's there? | **Quem é?**
[kɛj ɛ?]

Can I smoke here? | **Posso fumar aqui?**
['pɔsu fum'ar ak'i?]

May I ...? | **Posso ...?**
['pɔsu ...?]

Needs

I'd like ...	**Eu gostaria de ...** ['eu guʃtar'ia dɛ ...]
I don't want ...	**Eu não quero ...** ['eu 'nau 'kɛru ...]
I'm thirsty.	**Tenho sede.** ['tɛɲu 'sedɛ]
I want to sleep.	**Eu quero dormir.** ['eu 'kɛru durm'ir]
I want ...	**Eu queria ...** ['eu kɛr'ia ...]
to wash up	**lavar-me** [lav'armɛ]
to brush my teeth	**escovar os dentes** [ɛʃkuv'ar uʃ 'dẽtɛʃ]
to rest a while	**descansar um pouco** [dɛʃkãs'ar ũ 'poku]
to change my clothes	**trocar de roupa** [truk'ar dɛ 'ropa]
to go back to the hotel	**voltar ao hotel** [vɔlt'ar 'au ɔt'ɛl]
to buy ...	**comprar ...** [kõpr'ar ...]
to go to ...	**ir para ...** [ir 'para ...]
to visit ...	**visitar ...** [vizit'ar ...]
to meet with ...	**encontrar-me com ...** [ẽkõtr'armɛ kõ ...]
to make a call	**fazer uma chamada** [faz'er 'uma ʃam'ada]
I'm tired.	**Estou cansado /cansada/.** [ʃto kãs'adu /kãs'ada/]
We are tired.	**Nós estamos cansados /cansadas/.** [nɔʃ ɛʃt'amuʃ kãs'aduʃ /kãs'adaʃ/]
I'm cold.	**Tenho frio.** ['tɛɲu fr'iu]
I'm hot.	**Tenho calor.** ['tɛɲu kal'or]
I'm OK.	**Estou bem.** [ʃto bɛj]

I need to make a call.

Preciso de telefonar.
[prɛs'izu dɛ tɛlɛfun'ar]

I need to go to the restroom.

Preciso de ir à casa de banho.
[prɛs'izu dɛ ir a 'kaza dɛ 'baɲu]

I have to go.

Tenho de ir.
['tɛɲu dɛ ir]

I have to go now.

Tenho de ir agora.
['tɛɲu dɛ ir ag'ɔra]

Asking for directions

Excuse me, …

Desculpe, …
[dɛʃk'ulpɛ, …]

Where is …?

Onde fica …?
['õdɛ 'fika …?]

Which way is …?

Para que lado fica …?
['para kɛ 'ladu 'fika …?]

Could you help me, please?

Pode-me dar uma ajuda?
['pɔdɛmɛ dar 'uma aʒ'uda?]

I'm looking for …

Estou à procura de …
[ʃto a prɔk'ura dɛ …]

I'm looking for the exit.

Estou à procura da saída.
[ʃto a prɔk'ura da sa'ida]

I'm going to …

Eu vou para …
['eu vo 'para …]

Am I going the right way to …?

Estou a ir bem para …?
[ʃto a ir bɛj 'para …?]

Is it far?

Fica longe?
[f'ika 'lõʒɛ?]

Can I get there on foot?

Posso ir até lá a pé?
['pɔsu ir atɛ la a pɛ?]

Can you show me on the map?

Pode-me mostrar no mapa?
['pɔdɛmɛ muʃtr'ar nu 'mapa?]

Show me where we are right now.

Mostre-me onde estamos de momento.
['mɔʃtrɛmɛ 'õdɛ ɛʃt'amuʃ dɛ mum'ẽtu]

Here

Aqui
[ak'i]

There

Ali
[al'i]

This way

Por aqui
[pur ak'i]

Turn right.

Vire à direita.
['virɛ a dir'ɛjta]

Turn left.

Vire à esquerda.
['virɛ a ɛʃk'erda]

first (second, third) turn

primeira (segunda, terceira) curva
[prim'ɛjra (sɛg'ũda, tɛrs'ɛjra) 'kurva]

to the right

para a direita
['para a dir'ɛjta]

to the left   **para a esquerda**
                               ['para a ɛʃk'erda]

Go straight.   **Vá sempre em frente.**
                               [va 'sẽprɛ ɛj fr'ẽtɛ]

Signs

WELCOME!	**BEM-VINDOS!** [bɛjvˈiduʃ]
ENTRANCE	**ENTRADA** [ẽtrˈada]
EXIT	**SAÍDA** [saˈida]
PUSH	**EMPURRAR** [ẽpurˈar]
PULL	**PUXAR** [puʃˈar]
OPEN	**ABERTO** [abˈɛrtu]
CLOSED	**FECHADO** [fɛʃˈadu]
FOR WOMEN	**PARA SENHORAS** [ˈpara sɛɲˈoraʃ]
FOR MEN	**PARA HOMENS** [ˈpara ˈɔmɛjʃ]
MEN, GENTS	**HOMENS, CAVALHEIROS (M)** [ˈɔmɛjʃ, kavaʎˈɛjruʃ]
WOMEN, LADIES	**SENHORAS (F)** [sɛɲˈoraʃ]
DISCOUNTS	**DESCONTOS** [dɛʃkˈõtuʃ]
SALE	**SALDOS** [ˈsalduʃ]
FREE	**GRATUITO** [gratˈuitu]
NEW!	**NOVIDADE!** [nuvidˈadɛ!]
ATTENTION!	**ATENÇÃO!** [atẽsˈau!]
NO VACANCIES	**NÃO HÁ VAGAS** [ˈnau a ˈvagaʃ]
RESERVED	**RESERVADO** [rɛzɛrvˈadu]
ADMINISTRATION	**ADMINISTRAÇÃO** [adminiʃtrasˈau]
STAFF ONLY	**ACESSO RESERVADO** [asˈɛsu rɛzɛrvˈadu]

BEWARE OF THE DOG!	**CUIDADO COM O CÃO**
	[kuid'adu kõ u 'kau]
NO SMOKING!	**NÃO FUMAR!**
	['nau fum'ar!]
DO NOT TOUCH!	**NÃO MEXER!**
	['nau mɛʃer!]
DANGEROUS	**PERIGOSO**
	[pɛrig'ozu]
DANGER	**PERIGO**
	[pɛr'igu]
HIGH VOLTAGE	**ALTA TENSÃO**
	['alta tẽs'au]
NO SWIMMING!	**PROIBIDO NADAR**
	[pruib'idu nad'ar]

OUT OF ORDER	**FORA DE SERVIÇO**
	[fʲora dɛ sɛrv'isu]
FLAMMABLE	**INFLAMÁVEL**
	[iflam'avɛl]
FORBIDDEN	**PROIBIDO**
	[pruib'idu]
NO TRESPASSING!	**PASSAGEM PROIBIDA**
	[pas'aʒɛj pruib'ida]
WET PAINT	**PINTADO DE FRESCO**
	[p̃it'adu dɛ fr'eʃku]

CLOSED FOR RENOVATIONS	**FECHADO PARA OBRAS**
	[fɛʃadu 'para 'ɔbraʃ]
WORKS AHEAD	**TRABALHOS NA VIA**
	[trab'aʎuʃ na 'via]
DETOUR	**DESVIO**
	[dɛʒv'iu]

Transportation. General phrases

plane	**avião**
	[avj'au]
train	**comboio**
	[kõb'ɔju]
bus	**autocarro**
	[autɔk'aru]
ferry	**ferri**
	[fɛri]
taxi	**táxi**
	['taksi]
car	**carro**
	['karu]

schedule	**horário**
	[ɔr'ariu]
Where can I see the schedule?	**Onde posso ver o horário?**
	['õdɛ 'pɔsu ver u ɔr'ariu?]
workdays (weekdays)	**dias de trabalho**
	['diaʃ dɛ trab'aʎu]
weekends	**fins de semana**
	[fiʃ dɛ sɛm'ana]
holidays	**férias**
	[f'ɛriaʃ]

DEPARTURE	**PARTIDA**
	[part'ida]
ARRIVAL	**CHEGADA**
	[ʃɛg'ada]
DELAYED	**ATRASADO**
	[atraz'adu]
CANCELED	**CANCELADO**
	[kãsɛl'adu]

next (train, etc.)	**próximo**
	[pr'ɔsimu]
first	**primeiro**
	[prim'ɛjru]
last	**último**
	['ultimu]

When is the next ...?	**Quando é o próximo ...?**
	[ku'ãdu ɛ u pr'ɔsimu ...?]
When is the first ...?	**Quando é o primeiro ...?**
	[ku'ãdu ɛ u prim'ɛjru ...?]

When is the last ...?

Quando é o último ...?
[ku'ãdu ɛ u 'ultimu ...?]

transfer (change of trains, etc.)

transbordo
[trãʒb'ordu]

to make a transfer

fazer o transbordo
[faz'er u trãʒb'ordu]

Do I need to make a transfer?

Preciso de fazer o transbordo?
[prɛs'izu dɛ faz'er u trãʒb'ordu?]

Buying tickets

Where can I buy tickets?	**Onde posso comprar bilhetes?** ['õdɛ 'pɔsu kõpr'ar biʎ'etɛʃ?]
ticket	**bilhete** [biʎ'etɛ]
to buy a ticket	**comprar um bilhete** [kõpr'ar ũ biʎ'etɛ]
ticket price	**preço do bilhete** [pr'esu du biʎ'etɛ]
Where to?	**Para onde?** ['para 'õdɛ?]
To what station?	**Para que estação?** ['para kɛ ɛʃtas'au?]
I need ...	**Preciso de ...** [prɛs'izu dɛ ...]
one ticket	**um bilhete** [ũ biʎ'etɛ]
two tickets	**dois bilhetes** ['dojʃ biʎ'etɛʃ]
three tickets	**três bilhetes** [treʃ biʎ'etɛʃ]
one-way	**só de ida** [sɔ dɛ 'ida]
round-trip	**de ida e volta** [dɛ 'ida i 'vɔlta]
first class	**primeira classe** [prim'ɛjra kl'asɛ]
second class	**segunda classe** [sɛg'ũda kl'asɛ]
today	**hoje** ['oʒɛ]
tomorrow	**amanhã** [amaɲ'ã]
the day after tomorrow	**depois de amanhã** [dɛp'ojʃ dɛ amaɲ'ã]
in the morning	**de manhã** [dɛ maɲ'ã]
in the afternoon	**à tarde** [a 'tardɛ]
in the evening	**ao fim da tarde** ['au fi da 'tardɛ]

aisle seat	**lugar de corredor** [lug'ar dɛ kurɛd'or]
window seat	**lugar à janela** [lug'ar a ʒan'ɛla]
How much?	**Quanto?** [ku'ãtu?]
Can I pay by credit card?	**Posso pagar com cartão de crédito?** ['pɔsu pag'ar kõ kart'au dɛ kr'ɛditu?]

Bus

bus	**autocarro** [autɔk'aru]
intercity bus	**camioneta** [kamiun'ɛta]
bus stop	**paragem de autocarro** [par'aʒɛj dɛ autɔk'aru]
Where's the nearest bus stop?	**Onde é a paragem de autocarro mais perto?** ['õdɛ ɛ a par'aʒɛj dɛ autɔk'aru majʃ 'pɛrtu?]

number (bus ~, etc.)	**número** ['numɛru]
Which bus do I take to get to ...?	**Qual o autocarro que apanho para ...?** [ku'al u autɔk'aru kɛ ap'aɲu 'para ...?]
Does this bus go to ...?	**Este autocarro vai até ...?** ['eʃtɛ autɔk'aru vaj atɛ ...?]
How frequent are the buses?	**Com que frequência passam os autocarros?** [kõ kɛ frɛku'ẽsia 'pasau uʃ autɔk'aruʃ?]

every 15 minutes	**de 15 em 15 minutos** [dɛ 'k͡ïzɛ ɛj 'k͡ïzɛ min'utuʃ]
every half hour	**de meia em meia hora** [dɛ 'mɛja ɛj 'mɛja 'ɔra]
every hour	**de hora a hora** [dɛ 'ɔra a 'ɔra]
several times a day	**várias vezes ao dia** ['variaʃ 'vezɛʃ 'au dia]
... times a day	**... vezes ao dia** [... 'vezɛʃ 'au dia]

schedule	**horário** [ɔr'ariu]
Where can I see the schedule?	**Onde posso ver o horário?** ['õdɛ 'pɔsu ver u ɔr'ariu?]
When is the next bus?	**Quando é o próximo autocarro?** [ku'ãdu ɛ u pr'ɔsimu autɔk'aru?]
When is the first bus?	**Quando é o primeiro autocarro?** [ku'ãdu ɛ u prim'ɛjru autɔk'aru?]
When is the last bus?	**Quando é o último autocarro?** [ku'ãdu ɛ u 'ultimu autɔk'aru?]

stop

paragem
[par'aʒɛj]

next stop

próxima paragem
[prɔsima par'aʒɛj]

last stop (terminus)

última paragem
['ultima par'aʒɛj]

Stop here, please.

Pare aqui, por favor.
['parɛ ak'i, pur fav'or]

Excuse me, this is my stop.

Desculpe, esta é a minha paragem.
[dɛʃk'ulpɛ, 'ɛʃta ɛ a 'miɲa par'aʒɛj]

Train

train	**comboio** [kõb'ɔju]
suburban train	**comboio sub-urbano** [kõb'ɔju suburb'anu]
long-distance train	**comboio de longa distância** [kõb'ɔju dɛ 'lõga diʃt'ãsia]
train station	**estação de comboio** [ɛʃtas'au dɛ kõb'ɔju]
Excuse me, where is the exit to the platform?	**Desculpe, onde fica a saída para a plataforma?** [dɛʃk'ulpɛ, 'õdɛ 'fika a sa'ida 'para a plataf'ɔrma?]

Does this train go to ...?	**Este comboio vai até ...?** ['eʃtɛ kõb'ɔju vaj atɛ ...?]
next train	**próximo comboio** [pr'ɔsimu kõb'ɔju]
When is the next train?	**Quando é o próximo comboio?** [ku'ãdu ɛ u pr'ɔsimu kõb'ɔju?]
Where can I see the schedule?	**Onde posso ver o horário?** ['õdɛ 'pɔsu ver u ɔr'ariu?]
From which platform?	**Apartir de que plataforma?** [apart'ir dɛ kɛ plataf'ɔrma?]
When does the train arrive in ...?	**Quando é que o comboio chega a ...?** [ku'ãdu ɛ kɛ u kõb'ɔju ʃega a ...?]

Please help me.	**Ajude-me, por favor.** [aʒ'udɛmɛ, pur fav'or]
I'm looking for my seat.	**Estou à procura do meu lugar.** [ʃto a prɔk'ura du 'meu lug'ar]
We're looking for our seats.	**Nós estamos à procura dos nossos lugares.** [nɔʃ ɛʃt'amuʃ a prɔk'ura duʃ 'nɔsuʃ lug'arɛʃ]

My seat is taken.	**O meu lugar está ocupado.** [u 'meu lug'ar ɛʃt'a ɔkup'adu]
Our seats are taken.	**Os nossos lugares estão ocupados.** [uʃ 'nɔsuʃ lug'arɛʃ ɛʃt'au ɔkup'aduʃ]
I'm sorry but this is my seat.	**Peço desculpa mas este é o meu lugar.** ['pɛsu dɛʃk'ulpa maʃ 'eʃtɛ ɛ u 'meu lug'ar]

Is this seat taken?   **Este lugar está ocupado?**
                             ['eʃtɛ lug'ar ɛʃt'a ɔkup'adu?]

May I sit here?   **Posso sentar-me aqui?**
                             ['pɔsu sẽt'armɛ ak'i?]

On the train. Dialogue (No ticket)

Ticket, please.

Bilhete, por favor.
[biʎ'etɛ, pur fav'or]

I don't have a ticket.

Não tenho bilhete.
['nau 'tɛɲu biʎ'etɛ]

I lost my ticket.

Perdi o meu bilhete.
[pɛrd'i u 'meu biʎ'etɛ]

I forgot my ticket at home.

Esqueci-me do bilhete em casa.
[ɛʃkɛs'imɛ du biʎ'etɛ ɛj 'kaza]

You can buy a ticket from me.

Pode comprar um bilhete a mim.
['podɛ kõpr'ar ũ biʎ'etɛ a 'mĩ]

You will also have to pay a fine.

Terá também de pagar uma multa.
[tɛr'a tãb'ɛj dɛ pag'ar 'uma 'multa]

Okay.

Está bem.
[ɛʃt'a bɛj]

Where are you going?

Onde vai?
['õdɛ vaj?]

I'm going to ...

Eu vou para ...
['eu vo 'para ...]

How much? I don't understand.

Quanto é? Eu não entendo.
[ku'ãtu 'ɛ? 'eu 'nau ẽt'ẽdu]

Write it down, please.

Escreva, por favor.
[ɛʃkr'eva, pur fav'or]

Okay. Can I pay with a credit card?

Está bem. Posso pagar com cartão de crédito?
[ɛʃt'a bɛj. 'posu pag'ar kõ kart'au dɛ kr'ɛditu]

Yes, you can.

Sim, pode.
[sĩ, 'podɛ]

Here's your receipt.

Aqui tem a sua fatura.
[ak'i tɛj a 'sua fat'ura]

Sorry about the fine.

Desculpe pela multa.
[dɛʃk'ulpɛ 'pela 'multa]

That's okay. It was my fault.

Não tem mal. A culpa foi minha.
['nau tɛj mal. a 'kulpa 'foj 'miɲa]

Enjoy your trip.

Desfrute da sua viagem.
[dɛʃfr'utɛ da 'sua vj'aʒɛj]

Taxi

taxi
táxi
['taksi]

taxi driver
taxista
[taks'iʃta]

to catch a taxi
apanhar um táxi
[apaɲ'ar ũ 'taksi]

taxi stand
paragem de táxis
[par'aʒɛj dɛ 'taksiʃ]

Where can I get a taxi?
Onde posso apanhar um táxi?
['õdɛ 'pɔsu apaɲ'ar ũ 'taksi?]

to call a taxi
chamar um táxi
[ʃam'ar ũ 'taksi]

I need a taxi.
Preciso de um táxi.
[prɛs'izu dɛ ũ 'taksi]

Right now.
Agora.
[ag'ɔra]

What is your address (location)?
Qual é a sua morada?
[ku'al ɛ a 'sua mur'ada?]

My address is ...
A minha morada é ...
[a 'miɲa mur'ada ɛ ...]

Your destination?
Qual o seu destino?
[ku'al u 'seu dɛʃt'inu?]

Excuse me, ...
Desculpe, ...
[dɛʃk'ulpɛ, ...]

Are you available?
Está livre?
[ɛʃt'a 'livrɛ?]

How much is it to get to ...?
Em quanto fica a corrida até ...?
[ɛj ku'ãtu 'fika a kur'ida atɛ ...?]

Do you know where it is?
Sabe onde é?
['sabɛ 'õdɛ ɛ?]

Airport, please.
Para o aeroporto, por favor.
['para u aɛrɔp'ortu, pur fav'or]

Stop here, please.
Pare aqui, por favor.
['parɛ ak'i, pur fav'or]

It's not here.
Não é aqui.
['nau ɛ ak'i]

This is the wrong address.
Esta morada está errada.
['ɛʃta mur'ada ɛʃt'a ir'ada]

Turn left.
Vire à esquerda.
['virɛ a ɛʃk'erda]

Turn right.
Vire à direita.
['virɛ a dir'ɛjta]

How much do I owe you?

Quanto lhe devo?
[ku'ãtu ʎɛ 'devu?]

I'd like a receipt, please.

Queria fatura, por favor.
[kɛr'ia fat'ura, pur fav'or]

Keep the change.

Fique com o troco.
[f'ikɛ kõ u tr'oku]

Would you please wait for me?

Espere por mim, por favor.
[ɛʃp'ɛrɛ pur mĩ, pur fav'or]

five minutes

5 minutos
['sĩku min'utuʃ]

ten minutes

10 minutos
[dɛʃ min'utuʃ]

fifteen minutes

15 minutos
['kĩzɛ min'utuʃ]

twenty minutes

20 minutos
['vĩtɛ min'utuʃ]

half an hour

meia hora
['mɛja 'ɔra]

Hotel

Hello.	**Olá!** [ɔl'a!]
My name is …	**Chamo-me …** [ˈʃamumɛ …]
I have a reservation.	**Tenho uma reserva.** [ˈtɐɲu ˈuma rɛzˈɛrva]
I need …	**Preciso de …** [prɛsˈizu dɛ …]
a single room	**um quarto de solteiro** [ũ kuˈartu dɛ sɔltˈɛjru]
a double room	**um quarto de casal** [ũ kuˈartu dɛ kazˈal]
How much is that?	**Quanto é?** [kuˈãtu ˈɛ?]
That's a bit expensive.	**Está um pouco caro.** [ɛʃtˈa ũ ˈpoku ˈkaru]
Do you have any other options?	**Não tem outras opções?** [ˈnau tɛj ˈotraʃ ɔpsˈõjʃ?]
I'll take it.	**Eu fico com ele.** [ˈeu ˈfiku kõ ˈɛle]
I'll pay in cash.	**Eu pago em dinheiro.** [ˈeu ˈpagu ɛj diɲˈɛjru]
I've got a problem.	**Tenho um problema.** [ˈtɛɲu ũ prublˈema]
My … is broken.	**O meu … está partido** **/A minha … está partida/.** [u ˈmeu … ɛʃtˈa partˈidu /a ˈmiɲa … ɛʃtˈa partˈida/]
My … is out of order.	**O meu … está avariado** **/A minha … está avariada/.** [u ˈmeu … ɛʃtˈa avarjˈadu /a ˈmiɲa … ɛʃtˈa avarjˈada/]
TV	**televisor (m)** [tɛlɛvizˈor]
air conditioning	**ar condicionado (m)** [ar kõdisiunˈadu]
tap	**torneira (f)** [turnˈɛjra]
shower	**duche (m)** [ˈduʃɛ]

sink	**lavatório (m)** [lavat'ɔriu]
safe	**cofre (m)** ['kɔfrɛ]
door lock	**fechadura (f)** [fɛʃad'ura]
electrical outlet	**tomada elétrica (f)** [tum'ada el'ɛtrika]
hairdryer	**secador de cabelo (m)** [sɛkad'or dɛ kab'elu]

I don't have ...	**Não tenho ...** ['nau 'tɛɲu ...]
water	**água** ['agua]
light	**luz** [luʃ]
electricity	**eletricidade** [elɛtrisid'adɛ]

Can you give me ...?	**Pode dar-me ...?** ['pɔdɛ darmɛ ...?]
a towel	**uma toalha** ['uma tu'aʎa]
a blanket	**um cobertor** [ũ kubɛrt'or]
slippers	**uns chinelos** [ũʃ ʃin'ɛluʃ]
a robe	**um roupão** [ũ rop'au]
shampoo	**algum champô** [alg'ũ ʃãp'o]
soap	**algum sabonete** [alg'ũ sabun'etɛ]

I'd like to change rooms.	**Gostaria de trocar de quartos.** [guʃtar'ia dɛ truk'ar dɛ ku'artuʃ]
I can't find my key.	**Não consigo encontrar a minha chave.** ['nau kõs'igu ẽkõtr'ar a 'miɲa ʃ'avɛ]
Could you open my room, please?	**Abra-me o quarto, por favor.** ['abramɛ u ku'artu, pur fav'or]

Who's there?	**Quem é?** [kɛj ɛ?]
Come in!	**Entre!** [ẽtrɛ!]
Just a minute!	**Um minuto!** [ũ min'utu!]
Not right now, please.	**Agora não, por favor.** [ag'ɔra 'nau, pur fav'or]
Come to my room, please.	**Venha ao meu quarto, por favor.** ['vɛɲa 'au 'meu ku'artu, pur fav'or]

I'd like to order food service.

Gostaria de encomendar comida.
[guʃtar'ia dɛ ẽkumẽd'ar kum'ida]

My room number is ...

O número do meu quarto é ...
[u 'numɛru du 'meu ku'artu ɛ ...]

I'm leaving ...

Estou de saída ...
[ʃto dɛ sa'ida ...]

We're leaving ...

Estamos de saída ...
[ʃt'amuʃ dɛ sa'ida ...]

right now

agora
[ag'ɔra]

this afternoon

esta tarde
['ɛʃta 'tardɛ]

tonight

hoje à noite
['oʒɛ a 'nojtɛ]

tomorrow

amanhã
[amaɲ'ã]

tomorrow morning

amanhã de manhã
[amaɲ'ã dɛ maɲ'ã]

tomorrow evening

amanhã ao fim da tarde
[amaɲ'ã 'au fi da 'tardɛ]

the day after tomorrow

depois de amanhã
[dɛp'ojʃ dɛ amaɲ'ã]

I'd like to pay.

Gostaria de pagar.
[guʃtar'ia dɛ pag'ar]

Everything was wonderful.

Estava tudo maravilhoso.
[ɛʃt'ava 'tudu maraviʎ'ozu]

Where can I get a taxi?

Onde posso apanhar um táxi?
['õdɛ 'posu apaɲ'ar ũ 'taksi?]

Would you call a taxi for me, please?

Pode me chamar um táxi, por favor?
['podɛ mɛ ʃam'ar ũ 'taksi, pur fav'or]

Restaurant

Can I look at the menu, please?
Posso ver o menu, por favor?
['pɔsu 'ver u mɛn'u, pur fav'or?]

Table for one.
Mesa para um.
['meza 'para ũ]

There are two (three, four) of us.
Somos dois (três, quatro).
['somuʃ dojʃ (treʃ, ku'atru)]

Smoking
Para fumadores
['para fumad'orɛʃ]

No smoking
Para não fumadores
['para 'nau fumad'orɛʃ]

Excuse me! (addressing a waiter)
Por favor!
[pur fav'or!]

menu
menu
[mɛn'u]

wine list
lista de vinhos
['liʃta dɛ 'viɲuʃ]

The menu, please.
O menu, por favor.
[u mɛn'u, pur fav'or]

Are you ready to order?
Já escolheu?
[ʒa eʃkuʎ'eu?]

What will you have?
O que vai tomar?
[u kɛ vaj tum'ar?]

I'll have …
Eu quero …
['eu 'kɛru …]

I'm a vegetarian.
Eu sou vegetariano /vegetariana/.
['eu so vɛʒɛtarj'anu /vɛʒɛtarj'ana/]

meat
carne
['karnɛ]

fish
peixe
['pɛjʃɛ]

vegetables
vegetais
[vɛʒɛt'ajʃ]

Do you have vegetarian dishes?
Tem pratos vegetarianos?
[tɛj pr'atuʃ vɛʒɛtarj'anuʃ?]

I don't eat pork.
Não como porco.
['nau 'komu 'porku]

He /she/ doesn't eat meat.
Ele /ela/ não come porco.
['ɛle /'ɛla/ 'nau 'kɔmɛ 'porku]

I am allergic to …
Sou alérgico /alérgica/ a …
[so al'ɛrʒiku /al'ɛrʒika/ a …]

Would you please bring me …	**Por favor, pode trazer-me …?** [pur fav'or, 'pɔdɛ traz'ɛrmɛ …?]
salt | pepper | sugar	**sal | pimenta | açúcar** [sal | pim'ẽta | as'ukar]
coffee | tea | dessert	**café | chá | sobremesa** [kaf'ɛ | ʃa | sobrɛm'eza]
water | sparkling | plain	**água | com gás | sem gás** ['agua | kõ gaʃ | sɛj gaʃ]
a spoon | fork | knife	**uma colher | um garfo | uma faca** ['uma kuʎ'ɛr | ũ 'garfu | uma 'faka]
a plate | napkin	**um prato | um guardanapo** [ũ pr'atu | ũ guardan'apu]

Enjoy your meal!	**Bom apetite!** [bõ apɛt'itɛ!]
One more, please.	**Mais um, por favor.** ['maiʃ ũ, pur fav'or]
It was very delicious.	**Estava delicioso.** [ɛʃt'ava dɛlisj'ozu]

check | change | tip	**conta | troco | gorjeta** ['kõta | tr'oku | gurʒ'eta]
Check, please. (Could I have the check, please?)	**A conta, por favor.** [a 'kõta, pur fav'or]
Can I pay by credit card?	**Posso pagar com cartão de crédito?** ['pɔsu pag'ar kõ kart'au dɛ kr'ɛditu?]
I'm sorry, there's a mistake here.	**Desculpe, mas tem um erro aqui.** [dɛʃk'ulpɛ, maʃ tɛj ũ 'eru ak'i]

Shopping

Can I help you?

Posso ajudá-lo /ajudá-la/?
['pɔsu aʒud'alu /aʒud'ala/?]

Do you have ...?

Tem ...?
[tɛj ...?]

I'm looking for ...

Estou à procura de ...
[ʃto a prɔk'ura dɛ ...]

I need ...

Preciso de ...
[prɛs'izu dɛ ...]

I'm just looking.

Estou só a ver.
[ʃto sɔ a ver]

We're just looking.

Estamos só a ver.
[ɛʃt'amuʃ sɔ a ver]

I'll come back later.

Volto mais tarde.
['vɔltu 'maiʃ 'tardɛ]

We'll come back later.

Voltamos mais tarde.
[vɔlt'amuʃ 'maiʃ 'tardɛ]

discounts | sale

descontos | saldos
[dɛʃk'õtuʃ | 'salduʃ]

Would you please show me ...

Mostre-me, por favor ...
['mɔʃtrɛmɛ, pur fav'or ...]

Would you please give me ...

Dê-me, por favor ...
['demɛ, pur fav'or ...]

Can I try it on?

Posso experimentar?
['pɔsu ɛʃpɛrimẽt'ar?]

Excuse me, where's the fitting room?

**Desculpe, onde fica
a cabine de prova?**
[dɛʃk'ulpɛ, 'õdɛ 'fika
a kab'inɛ dɛ pr'ɔva?]

Which color would you like?

Que cor prefere?
[kɛ kor prɛf'ɛrɛ?]

size | length

tamanho | comprimento
[tam'aɲu | kõprim'ẽtu]

How does it fit?

Como lhe fica?
['komu ʎɛ 'fika?]

How much is it?

Quanto é que isto custa?
[ku'ãtu ɛ kɛ 'iʃtu 'kuʃta?]

That's too expensive.

É muito caro.
[ɛ 'muitu 'karu]

I'll take it.

Eu fico com ele.
['eu 'fiku kõ 'ɛle]

Excuse me, where do I pay?

Desculpe, onde fica a caixa?
[dɛʃk'ulpɛ, 'õdɛ 'fika a 'kajʃa?]

Will you pay in cash or credit card?

Vai pagar a dinheiro ou com cartão de crédito?
[vaj pag'ar a diɲ'ɛjru o kõ kart'au dɛ kr'ɛditu?]

In cash | with credit card

A dinheiro | com cartão de crédito
[a diɲ'ɛjru | kõ kart'au dɛ kr'ɛditu]

Do you want the receipt?

Pretende fatura?
[prɛt'ẽdɛ fat'ura?]

Yes, please.

Sim, por favor.
[sĩ, pur fav'or]

No, it's OK.

Não. Está bem!
['nau. ɛʃt'a bɛj]

Thank you. Have a nice day!

Obrigado /Obrigada/.
Tenha um bom dia!
[ɔbrig'adu /ɔbrig'ada/. 'taɲa ũ bõ 'dia!]

In town

Excuse me, please.	**Desculpe, por favor ...** [dɛʃk'ulpɛ, pur fav'or ...]
I'm looking for ...	**Estou à procura ...** [ʃto a prɔk'ura ...]
the subway	**do metro** [du 'mɛtru]
my hotel	**do meu hotel** [du 'meu ɔt'ɛl]
the movie theater	**do cinema** [du sin'ema]
a taxi stand	**da praça de táxis** [da pr'asa dɛ 'taksiʃ]

an ATM	**do multibanco** [du multib'ãku]
a foreign exchange office	**de uma casa de câmbio** [dɛ 'uma 'kaza dɛ 'kãbiu]
an internet café	**de um café internet** [dɛ ũ kafɛˈĩtɛrn'ɛtɛ]
... street	**da rua ...** [da 'rua ...]
this place	**deste lugar** ['deʃtɛ lug'ar]

Do you know where ... is?	**Sabe dizer-me onde fica ...?** ['sabɛ diz'ermɛ 'õdɛ 'fika ...?]
Which street is this?	**Como se chama esta rua?** ['komu sɛ ʃ'ama 'ɛʃta 'rua?]
Show me where we are right now.	**Mostre-me onde estamos de momento.** ['mɔʃtrɛmɛ 'õdɛ ɛʃt'amuʃ dɛ mum'ẽtu]
Can I get there on foot?	**Posso ir até lá a pé?** ['pɔsu ir atɛ la a pɛ?]
Do you have a map of the city?	**Tem algum mapa da cidade?** [tɛj alg'ũ 'mapa da sid'adɛ?]

How much is a ticket to get in?	**Quanto custa a entrada?** [ku'ãtu 'kuʃta a ẽtr'ada?]
Can I take pictures here?	**Pode-se fotografar aqui?** ['pɔdɛsɛ futugraf'ar ak'i?]
Are you open?	**Estão abertos?** [ɛʃt'au ab'ɛrtuʃ?]

When do you open?

A que horas abrem?
[a kɛ 'ɔraʃ 'abrɛj?]

When do you close?

A que horas fecham?
[a kɛ 'ɔraʃ 'faʃau?]

Money

money	**dinheiro** [diɲ'ɛjru]
cash	**a dinheiro** [a diɲ'ɛjru]
paper money	**dinheiro de papel** [diɲ'ɛjru dɛ pap'ɛl]
loose change	**troco** [tr'oku]
check | change | tip	**conta | troco | gorjeta** ['kõta | tr'oku | gurʒ'eta]
credit card	**cartão de crédito** [kart'au dɛ kr'ɛditu]
wallet	**carteira** [kart'ɛjra]
to buy	**comprar** [kõpr'ar]
to pay	**pagar** [pag'ar]
fine	**multa** ['multa]
free	**gratuito** [grat'uitu]
Where can I buy ...?	**Onde é que posso comprar ...?** ['õdɛ ɛ kɛ 'pɔsu kõpr'ar ...?]
Is the bank open now?	**O banco está aberto agora?** [u 'bãku ɛʃt'a ab'ɛrtu ag'ɔra?]
When does it open?	**Quando abre?** [ku'ãdu 'abrɛ?]
When does it close?	**Quando fecha?** [ku'ãdu 'faʃa?]
How much?	**Quanto?** [ku'ãtu?]
How much is this?	**Quanto custa isto?** [ku'ãtu 'kuʃta 'iʃtu?]
That's too expensive.	**É muito caro.** [ɛ 'muitu 'karu]
Excuse me, where do I pay?	**Desculpe, onde fica a caixa?** [dɛʃk'ulpɛ, 'õdɛ 'fika a 'kajʃa?]
Check, please.	**A conta, por favor.** [a 'kõta, pur fav'or]

Can I pay by credit card? | **Posso pagar com cartão de crédito?**
['pɔsu pag'ar kõ kart'au dɛ kr'ɛditu?]

Is there an ATM here? | **Há algum Multibanco aqui?**
['a alg'ũ multib'äku ak'i?]

I'm looking for an ATM. | **Estou à procura de um Multibanco.**
[ʃto a prɔk'ura dɛ ũ multib'äku]

I'm looking for a foreign exchange office. | **Estou à procura de uma casa de câmbio.**
[ʃto a prɔk'ura dɛ 'uma 'kaza dɛ 'käbiu]

I'd like to change … | **Eu gostaria de trocar …**
['eu guʃtar'ia dɛ truk'ar …]

What is the exchange rate? | **Qual a taxa de câmbio?**
[ku'al a 'taʃa dɛ 'käbiu?]

Do you need my passport? | **Precisa do meu passaporte?**
[prɛs'iza du 'meu pasap'ɔrtɛ?]

Time

What time is it?	**Que horas são?** [kɛ 'oraʃ 'sau?]
When?	**Quando?** [ku'ãdu?]
At what time?	**A que horas?** [a kɛ 'oraʃ?]
now | later | after ...	**agora | mais tarde | depois ...** [ag'ora | 'maiʃ 'tardɛ | dɛp'ojʃ ...]

one o'clock	**uma em ponto** ['uma ɛj 'põtu]
one fifteen	**uma e quinze** ['uma i 'k̃izɛ]
one thirty	**uma e trinta** ['uma i tr̃ita]
one forty-five	**uma e quarenta e cinco** ['uma i kuar'ẽta i 's̃iku]

one | two | three	**um | dois | três** [ũ | 'dojʃ | treʃ]
four | five | six	**quatro | cinco | seis** [ku'atru | 's̃iku | 'sɛiʃ]
seven | eight | nine	**sete | oito | nove** ['sɛtɛ | 'ojtu | 'nɔvɛ]
ten | eleven | twelve	**dez | onze | doze** [dɛʃ | 'õzɛ | 'dozɛ]

in ...	**dentro de ...** ['dẽtru dɛ ...]
five minutes	**5 minutos** ['s̃iku min'utuʃ]
ten minutes	**10 minutos** [dɛʃ min'utuʃ]
fifteen minutes	**15 minutos** ['k̃izɛ min'utuʃ]
twenty minutes	**20 minutos** ['ṽitɛ min'utuʃ]

half an hour	**meia hora** ['mɛja 'ora]
an hour	**uma hora** ['uma 'ora]

in the morning — **de manhã**
[dɛ maɲ'ã]

early in the morning — **de manhã cedo**
[dɛ maɲ'ã 'sedu]

this morning — **esta manhã**
['ɛʃta maɲ'ã]

tomorrow morning — **amanhã de manhã**
[amaɲ'ã dɛ maɲ'ã]

at noon — **ao meio-dia**
['au mɛjud'ia]

in the afternoon — **à tarde**
[a 'tardɛ]

in the evening — **à noite**
[a 'nojtɛ]

tonight — **esta noite**
['ɛʃta 'nojtɛ]

at night — **à noite**
[a 'nojtɛ]

yesterday — **ontem**
['õtɛj uʃ]

today — **hoje**
['oʒɛ]

tomorrow — **amanhã**
[amaɲ'ã]

the day after tomorrow — **depois de amanhã**
[dɛp'ojʃ dɛ amaɲ'ã]

What day is it today? — **Que dia é hoje?**
[kɛ 'dia ɛ 'oʒɛ?]

It's ... — **Hoje é ...**
['oʒɛ ɛ ...]

Monday — **segunda-feira**
[sɛ'gũda 'fɛjra]

Tuesday — **terça-feira**
[tersa 'fɛjra]

Wednesday — **quarta-feira**
[kuarta 'fɛjra]

Thursday — **quinta-feira**
[k̃ita 'fɛjra]

Friday — **sexta-feira**
[saʃta 'fɛjra]

Saturday — **sábado**
['sabadu]

Sunday — **domingo**
[dum'ĩgu]

Greetings. Introductions

Hello.

Olá!
[ɔl'a!]

Pleased to meet you.

Prazer em conhecê-lo /conhecê-la/.
[praz'er ɛj kuɲɛs'elu /kuɲɛs'ela/]

Me too.

O prazer é todo meu.
[u praz'er ɛ 'todu 'meu]

I'd like you to meet ...

Apresento-lhe ...
[aprɛz'ẽtuʎɛ ...]

Nice to meet you.

Muito prazer.
['muitu praz'er]

How are you?

Como está?
['komu ɛʃt'a?]

My name is ...

Chamo-me ...
['ʃamumɛ ...]

His name is ...

Ele chama-se ...
['ɛle ʃ'amasɛ ...]

Her name is ...

Ela chama-se ...
['ɛla ʃ'amasɛ ...]

What's your name?

Como é que o senhor /a senhora/ se chama?
['komu ɛ kɛ u sɛɲ'or /a sɛɲ'ora/ sɛ ʃ'ama?]

What's his name?

Como é que ela se chama?
['komu ɛ kɛ 'ɛla sɛ ʃ'ama?]

What's her name?

Como é que ela se chama?
['komu ɛ kɛ 'ɛla sɛ ʃ'ama?]

What's your last name?

Qual o seu apelido?
[ku'al u 'seu apɛl'idu?]

You can call me ...

Pode chamar-me ...
['pɔdɛ ʃam'armɛ ...]

Where are you from?

De onde é?
[dɛ 'õdɛ ɛ?]

I'm from ...

Sou de ...
[so dɛ ...]

What do you do for a living?

O que faz na vida?
[u kɛ faʃ na 'vida?]

Who is this?

Quem é este?
[kɛj ɛ 'eʃtɛ?]

Who is he?

Quem é ele?
[kɛj ɛ 'ɛle?]

Who is she?

Quem é ela?
[kɛj ɛ 'ɛla?]

Who are they?

Quem são eles?
[kɛj 'sau 'ɛleʃ?]

This is ...

Este é ...
['eʃtɛ ɛ ...]

my friend (masc.)

o meu amigo
[u 'meu am'igu]

my friend (fem.)

a minha amiga
[a 'miɲa am'iga]

my husband

o meu marido
[u 'meu mar'idu]

my wife

a minha mulher
[a 'miɲa muʎ'ɛr]

my father

o meu pai
[u 'meu 'paj]

my mother

a minha mãe
[a 'miɲa mɛj]

my brother

o meu irmão
[u 'meu irm'au]

my sister

a minha irmã
[a 'miɲa irm'ã]

my son

o meu filho
[u 'meu 'fiʎu]

my daughter

a minha filha
[a 'miɲa 'fiʎa]

This is our son.

Este é o nosso filho.
['eʃtɛ ɛ u 'nɔsu 'fiʎu]

This is our daughter.

Este é a nossa filha.
['eʃtɛ ɛ a 'nɔsa 'fiʎa]

These are my children.

Estes são os meus filhos.
['eʃtɛʃ 'sau uʃ 'meuʃ 'fiʎuʃ]

These are our children.

Estes são os nossos filhos.
['eʃtɛʃ 'sau uʃ 'nɔsuʃ 'fiʎuʃ]

Farewells

Good bye!	**Adeus!** [ad'ɛuʃ]
Bye! (inform.)	**Tchau!** [tʃau!]
See you tomorrow.	**Até amanhã.** [at'ɛ amaɲ'ã]
See you soon.	**Até breve.** [at'ɛ br'ɛvɛ]
See you at seven.	**Até às sete.** [at'ɛ aʃ 'sɛtɛ]

Have fun!	**Diverte-te!** [div'ɛrtɛtɛ!]
Talk to you later.	**Falamos mais tarde.** [fal'amuʃ 'maiʃ 'tardɛ]
Have a nice weekend.	**Bom fim de semana.** [bõ fi dɛ sɛm'ana]
Good night.	**Boa noite.** ['boa 'nojtɛ]

It's time for me to go.	**Está na hora.** [ɛʃt'a na 'ɔra]
I have to go.	**Preciso de ir embora.** [prɛs'izu dɛ ir ɛ̃b'ɔra]
I will be right back.	**Volto já.** ['vɔltu ʒa]

It's late.	**Já é tarde.** [ʒa ɛ 'tardɛ]
I have to get up early.	**Tenho de me levantar cedo.** ['tɛɲu dɛ mɛ lɛvãt'ar 'sedu]
I'm leaving tomorrow.	**Vou-me embora amanhã.** ['vomɛ ɛ̃b'ɔra amaɲ'ã]
We're leaving tomorrow.	**Vamos embora amanhã.** ['vamuʃ ɛ̃b'ɔra amaɲ'ã]

Have a nice trip!	**Boa viagem!** ['boa vj'aʒɛj!]
It was nice meeting you.	**Tive muito prazer em conhecer-vos.** ['tivɛ 'muitu praz'er ɛj kuɲɛs'ervuʃ]
It was nice talking to you.	**Foi muito agradável falar consigo.** [foj 'muitu agrad'avɛl fal'ar kõs'igu]
Thanks for everything.	**Obrigado /Obrigada/ por tudo.** [ɔbrig'adu /ɔbrig'ada/ pur 'tudu]

I had a very good time.

Passei um tempo muito agradável.
[pas'ɛj ũ 'tẽpu 'muitu agrad'avɛl]

We had a very good time.

Passámos um tempo muito agradável.
[pas'amuʃ ũ 'tẽpu 'muitu agrad'avɛl]

It was really great.

Foi mesmo fantástico.
[foj 'meʒmu fãt'aʃtiku]

I'm going to miss you.

Vou ter saudades suas.
[vo ter saud'adɛʃ 'suaʃ]

We're going to miss you.

Vamos ter saudades suas.
['vamuʃ ter saud'adɛʃ 'suaʃ]

Good luck!

Boa sorte!
['boa 'sɔrtɛ!]

Say hi to …

Dê cumprimentos a …
[de kũprim'ẽtuʃ a …]

Foreign language

I don't understand.	**Eu não entendo.** ['eu 'nau ẽt'ẽdu]
Write it down, please.	**Escreva isso, por favor.** [ɛʃkr'eva 'isu, pur fav'or]
Do you speak ...?	**O senhor /a senhora/ fala ...?** [u sɛɲ'or /a sɛɲ'ora/ 'fala ...?]

I speak a little bit of ...	**Eu falo um pouco de ...** ['eu 'falu ũ 'poku dɛ ...]
English	**Inglês** [igl'eʃ]
Turkish	**Turco** ['turku]
Arabic	**Árabe** ['arabɛ]
French	**Francês** [frãs'eʃ]

German	**Alemão** [alɛm'au]
Italian	**Italiano** [italj'anu]
Spanish	**Espanhol** [ɛʃpaɲ'ɔl]
Portuguese	**Português** [purtug'eʃ]
Chinese	**Chinês** [ʃin'eʃ]
Japanese	**Japonês** [ʒapun'eʃ]

Can you repeat that, please.	**Pode repetir isso, por favor.** ['pɔdɛ rɛpɛt'ir 'isu, pur fav'or]
I understand.	**Compreendo.** [kõprj'ẽdu]
I don't understand.	**Eu não entendo.** ['eu 'nau ẽt'ẽdu]
Please speak more slowly.	**Por favor fale mais devagar.** [pur fav'or 'falɛ 'maiʃ dɛvag'ar]

Is that correct? (Am I saying it right?)	**Isso está certo?** ['isu ɛʃt'a 'sɛrtu?]
What is this? (What does this mean?)	**O que é isto?** [u kɛ ɛ 'iʃtu?]

Apologies

Excuse me, please.	**Desculpe-me, por favor.** [dɛʃkˈulpɛmɛ, pur favˈor]
I'm sorry.	**Lamento.** [lamˈẽtu]
I'm really sorry.	**Tenho muita pena.** ['tɛɲu 'muita 'pena]
Sorry, it's my fault.	**Desculpe, a culpa é minha.** [dɛʃkˈulpɛ, a ˈkulpa ɛ ˈmiɲa]
My mistake.	**O erro foi meu.** [u ˈeru foj ˈmeu]
May I ...?	**Posso ...?** [ˈpɔsu ...?]
Do you mind if I ...?	**O senhor /a senhora/ não se importa se eu ...?** [u sɛɲˈor /a sɛɲˈora/ ˈnau sɛ ĩpˈɔrta sɛ ˈeu ...?]
It's OK.	**Não faz mal.** [ˈnau faʃ mal]
It's all right.	**Está tudo em ordem.** [ɛʃtˈa ˈtudu ɛj ˈɔrdɛj]
Don't worry about it.	**Não se preocupe.** [ˈnau sɛ priɔkˈupɛ]

Agreement

Yes. **Sim.**
[sĩ]

Yes, sure. **Sim, claro.**
[sĩ, kl'aru]

OK (Good!) **Está bem!**
[ɛʃt'a bɛj!]

Very well. **Muito bem.**
['muitu bɛj]

Certainly! **Claro!**
[kl'aru!]

I agree. **Concordo.**
[kõk'ɔrdu]

That's correct. **Certo.**
['sɛrtu]

That's right. **Correto.**
[kur'ɛtu]

You're right. **Tem razão.**
[tɛj raz'au]

I don't mind. **Eu não me oponho.**
['eu 'nau mɛ ɔp'oɲu]

Absolutely right. **Absolutamente certo.**
[absulutam'ẽtɛ 'sɛrtu]

It's possible. **É possível.**
[ɛ pus'ivɛl]

That's a good idea. **É uma boa ideia.**
[ɛ 'uma 'boa id'ɛja]

I can't say no. **Não posso recusar.**
['nau 'pɔsu rɛkuz'ar]

I'd be happy to. **Terei muito gosto.**
[tɛr'ɛj 'muitu 'goʃtu]

With pleasure. **Com prazer.**
[kõ praz'er]

Refusal. Expressing doubt

No.
Não.
['nau]

Certainly not.
Claro que não.
[kl'aru kε 'nau]

I don't agree.
Não concordo.
['nau kõk'ɔrdu]

I don't think so.
Não creio.
['nau kr'εju]

It's not true.
Isso não é verdade.
['isu 'nau ε vεrd'adε]

You are wrong.
O senhor /a senhora/ não tem razão.
[u sεɲ'or /a sεɲ'ora/ 'nau tεj raz'au]

I think you are wrong.
Acho que o senhor /a senhora/ não tem razão.
['aʃu kε u sεɲ'or /a sεɲ'ora/ 'nau tεj raz'au]

I'm not sure.
Não tenho a certeza.
['nau 'tεɲu a sεrt'eza]

It's impossible.
É impossível.
[ε ‾ipus'ivεl]

Nothing of the kind (sort)!
De modo algum!
[dε 'mɔdu alg'ũ!]

The exact opposite.
Exatamente o contrário.
[ezatam'ẽtε u kõtr'ariu]

I'm against it.
Sou contra.
[so 'kõtra]

I don't care.
Não me importo.
['nau mε ‾ip'ɔrtu]

I have no idea.
Não faço ideia.
['nau 'fasu id'εja]

I doubt that.
Não creio.
['nau kr'εju]

Sorry, I can't.
Desculpe, mas não posso.
[dεʃk'ulpε, maʃ 'nau 'pɔsu]

Sorry, I don't want to.
Desculpe, mas não quero.
[dεʃk'ulpε, maʃ 'nau 'kεru]

Thank you, but I don't need this.
Desculpe, não quero isso.
[dεʃk'ulpε, 'nau 'kεru 'isu]

It's late.
Já é muito tarde.
[ʒa ε 'muitu 'tardε]

I have to get up early.

Tenho de me levantar cedo.
['tɐɲu dɛ mɛ lɛvɐ̃t'ar 'sedu]

I don't feel well.

Não me sinto bem.
['nau mɛ 'sĩtu bɛj]

Expressing gratitude

Thank you.

Obrigado /Obrigada/.
[ɔbrig'adu /ɔbrig'ada/]

Thank you very much.

Muito obrigado /obrigada/.
['muitu ɔbrig'adu /ɔbrig'ada/]

I really appreciate it.

Fico muito grato /grata/.
[f'iku 'muitu gr'atu /gr'ata/]

I'm really grateful to you.

Estou-lhe muito reconhecido.
[ʃtoʎɛ 'muitu rɛkuɲɛs'idu]

We are really grateful to you.

Estamos-lhe muito reconhecidos.
[ɛʃt'amuʒʎɛ 'muitu rɛkuɲɛs'iduʃ]

Thank you for your time.

Obrigado /Obrigada/ pelo seu tempo.
[ɔbrig'adu /ɔbrig'ada/ 'pelu 'seu 'tẽpu]

Thanks for everything.

Obrigado /Obrigada/ por tudo.
[ɔbrig'adu /ɔbrig'ada/ pur 'tudu]

Thank you for …

Obrigado /Obrigada/ …
[ɔbrig'adu /ɔbrig'ada/ …]

your help

… pela sua ajuda
[… 'pela 'sua aʒ'uda]

a nice time

… por este tempo bem passado
[… 'pur 'eʃtɛ 'tẽpu bɛj pas'adu]

a wonderful meal

… pela comida deliciosa
[… 'pela kum'ida dɛlisj'ɔza]

a pleasant evening

… por esta noite agradável
[… pur 'ɛʃta 'nojtɛ agrad'avɛl]

a wonderful day

… pelo dia maravilhoso
[… 'pelu 'dia maraviʎ'ozu]

an amazing journey

… pela jornada fantástica
[… 'pela ʒurn'ada fãt'aʃtika]

Don't mention it.

Não tem de quê.
['nau tɛj dɛ ke]

You are welcome.

Não precisa agradecer.
['nau prɛs'iza agradɛs'er]

Any time.

Disponha sempre.
[diʃp'oɲa 'sẽprɛ]

My pleasure.

Foi um prazer ajudar.
['foj ũ praz'er aʒud'ar]

Forget it. It's alright.

Esqueça isso.
[ɛʃk'esa 'isu]

Don't worry about it.

Não se preocupe.
['nau sɛ priɔk'upɛ]

Congratulations. Best wishes

Congratulations!	**Parabéns!** [parab'ɛjʃ!]
Happy birthday!	**Feliz aniversário!** [fɛl'iʃ anivɛrs'ariu!]
Merry Christmas!	**Feliz Natal!** [fɛl'iʃ nat'al!]
Happy New Year!	**Feliz Ano Novo!** [fɛl'iʃ 'anu 'novu!]
Happy Easter!	**Feliz Páscoa!** [fɛl'iʃ 'paʃkua!]
Happy Hanukkah!	**Feliz Hanukkah!** [fɛl'iʃ an'ukka!]
I'd like to propose a toast.	**Gostaria de fazer um brinde.** [guʃtar'ia dɛ faz'er ũ brⁱidɛ]
Cheers!	**Saúde!** [sa'udɛ!]
Let's drink to …!	**Bebamos a …!** [bɛb'amuʃ a …!]
To our success!	**Ao nosso sucesso!** [au 'nɔsu sus'ɛsu!]
To your success!	**Ao vosso sucesso!** [au 'vɔsu sus'ɛsu!]
Good luck!	**Boa sorte!** ['boa 'sɔrtɛ!]
Have a nice day!	**Tenha um bom dia!** ['tɛɲa ũ bõ 'dia!]
Have a good holiday!	**Tenha um bom feriado!** ['tɛɲa ũ bõ fɛrj'adu!]
Have a safe journey!	**Tenha uma viagem segura!** ['tɛɲa 'uma vj'aʒɛj sɛg'ura!]
I hope you get better soon!	**Espero que melhore em breve!** [ɛʃp'ɛru kɛ mɛʎ'ɔrɛ ɛj br'ɛvɛ!]

Socializing

Why are you sad?	**Porque é que está chateado /chateada/?** ['purkɛ ɛ kɛ ɛʃt'a ʃatj'adu /ʃatj'ada/?]
Smile! Cheer up!	**Sorria!** [sur'ia!]
Are you free tonight?	**Está livre esta noite?** [ɛʃt'a 'livrɛ 'ɛʃta 'nojtɛ?]
May I offer you a drink?	**Posso oferecer-lhe algo para beber?** ['pɔsu ɔfɛrɛs'erʎɛ 'algu 'para bɛb'er?]
Would you like to dance?	**Você quer dançar?** [vɔs'e kɛr dãs'ar?]
Let's go to the movies.	**Vamos ao cinema.** ['vamuʃ 'au sin'ema]
May I invite you to …?	**Gostaria de a convidar para ir …** [guʃtar'ia dɛ a kõvid'ar 'para ir …]
a restaurant	**ao restaurante** ['au rɛʃtaur'ãtɛ]
the movies	**ao cinema** ['au sin'ema]
the theater	**ao teatro** ['au te'atru]
go for a walk	**passear** [pase'ar]
At what time?	**A que horas?** [a kɛ 'ɔraʃ?]
tonight	**hoje à noite** ['oʒɛ a 'nojtɛ]
at six	**às 6 horas** [aʃ 'sajʃ 'ɔraʃ]
at seven	**às 7 horas** [aʃ 'sɛtɛ 'ɔraʃ]
at eight	**às 8 horas** [aʃ 'ojtu 'ɔraʃ]
at nine	**às 9 horas** [aʃ 'nɔvɛ 'ɔraʃ]
Do you like it here?	**Gosta deste local?** ['gɔʃta 'deʃtɛ luk'al?]
Are you here with someone?	**Está com alguém?** [ɛʃt'a kõ alg'ɐj?]

I'm with my friend.

Estou com o meu amigo.
[ʃto kõ u 'meu am'igu]

I'm with my friends.

Estou com os meus amigos.
[ʃto kõ uʃ 'meuʃ am'iguʃ]

No, I'm alone.

Não, estou sozinho /sozinha/.
['nau, εʃt'o sɔz'iɲu /sɔz'iɲa/]

Do you have a boyfriend?

Tens namorado?
[tεjʃ namur'adu?]

I have a boyfriend.

Tenho namorado.
['tεɲu namur'adu]

Do you have a girlfriend?

Tens namorada?
[tεjʃ namur'ada?]

I have a girlfriend.

Tenho namorada.
['tεɲu namur'ada]

Can I see you again?

Posso voltar a ver-te?
['pɔsu vɔlt'ar a 'vertε?]

Can I call you?

Posso ligar-te?
['pɔsu lig'artε?]

Call me. (Give me a call.)

Liga-me.
['ligamε]

What's your number?

Qual é o teu número?
[ku'al ε u 'teu 'numεru?]

I miss you.

Tenho saudades tuas.
['tεɲu saud'adεʃ 'tuaʃ]

You have a beautiful name.

Tem um nome muito bonito.
[tεj ũ 'nomε 'muitu bun'itu]

I love you.

Amo-te.
['amutε]

Will you marry me?

Quer casar comigo?
[kεr kaz'ar kum'igu?]

You're kidding!

Você está a brincar!
[vɔs'e εʃt'a a bɾik'ar!]

I'm just kidding.

Estou só a brincar.
[ʃto sɔ a bɾik'ar]

Are you serious?

Está a falar a sério?
[εʃt'a a fal'ar a 'sεriu?]

I'm serious.

Estou a falar a sério.
[ʃto a fal'ar a 'sεriu]

Really?!

De verdade?!
[dε vεrd'adε?!]

It's unbelievable!

Incrível!
[ĩkr'ivεl]

I don't believe you.

Não acredito.
['nau akrεd'itu]

I can't.

Não posso.
['nau 'pɔsu]

I don't know.

Não sei.
['nau sεj]

I don't understand you.

Please go away.

Leave me alone!

Não entendo o que está a dizer.
['nau ẽt'ẽdu u kɛ ɛʃt'a a diz'er]

Saia, por favor.
['saja, pur fav'or]

Deixe-me em paz!
['dajʃɛmɛ ɛj paʃ!]

I can't stand him.

You are disgusting!

I'll call the police!

Eu não o suporto.
['eu 'nau u sup'ɔrtu]

Você é detestável!
[vɔs'e ɛ dɛtɛʃt'avɛl!]

Vou chamar a polícia!
[vo ʃam'ar a pul'isia!]

Sharing impressions. Emotions

I like it.	**Gosto disto.** ['goʃtu 'diʃtu]
Very nice.	**É muito simpático.** [ɛ 'muitu sĩp'atiku]
That's great!	**Fixe!** [f'iʃɛ!]
It's not bad.	**Não é mau.** ['nau ɛ 'mau]
I don't like it.	**Não gosto disto.** ['nau 'goʃtu 'diʃtu]
It's not good.	**Isso não está certo.** ['isu 'nau ɛʃt'a 'sɛrtu]
It's bad.	**Isso é mau.** ['isu ɛ 'mau]
It's very bad.	**Isso é muito mau.** ['isu ɛ 'muitu 'mau]
It's disgusting.	**Isso é asqueroso.** ['isu ɛ aʃkɛr'ozu]
I'm happy.	**Estou feliz.** [ʃto fɛl'iʃ]
I'm content.	**Estou contente.** [ʃto kõt'ẽtɛ]
I'm in love.	**Estou apaixonado /apaixonada/.** [ʃto apajʃun'adu /apajʃun'ada/]
I'm calm.	**Estou calmo /calma/.** [ʃto 'kalmu /k'alma/]
I'm bored.	**Estou aborrecido /aborrecida/.** [ʃto aburɛs'idu /aburɛs'ida/]
I'm tired.	**Estou cansado /cansada/.** [ʃto kãs'adu /kãs'ada/]
I'm sad.	**Estou triste.** [ʃto tr'iʃtɛ]
I'm frightened.	**Estou apavorado /apavorada/.** [ʃto apavur'adu /apavur'ada/]
I'm angry.	**Estou zangado /zangada/.** [ʃto zãg'adu /zãg'ada/]
I'm worried.	**Estou preocupado /preocupada/.** [ʃto priɔkup'adu /priɔkup'ada/]
I'm nervous.	**Estou nervoso /nervosa/.** [ʃto nɛrv'ozu /nɛrv'ɔza/]

I'm jealous. (envious)

Estou ciumento /ciumenta/.
[ʃto sium'ẽtu /sium'ẽta/]

I'm surprised.

Estou surpreendido /surpreendida/.
[ʃto surpriẽd'idu /surpriẽd'ida/]

I'm perplexed.

Estou perplexo /perplexa/.
[ʃto pɛrpl'ɛksu /pɛrpl'ɛksa/]

Problems. Accidents

I've got a problem. | **Tenho um problema.**
['tɛɲu ũ prubl'ema]

We've got a problem. | **Temos um problema.**
['tɛmuʃ ũ prubl'ema]

I'm lost. | **Estou perdido.**
[ʃto pɛrd'idu]

I missed the last bus (train). | **Perdi o último autocarro (comboio).**
[pɛrd'i u 'ultimu autɔk'aru (kõb'ɔju).]

I don't have any money left. | **Não me resta nenhum dinheiro.**
['nau mɛ 'rɛʃta nɛɲ'ũ diɲ'ɛjru]

I've lost my ... | **Eu perdi ...**
['eu pɛrd'i ...]

Someone stole my ... | **Roubaram-me ...**
[rob'araumɛ ...]

passport | **o meu passaporte**
[u 'meu pasap'ɔrtɛ]

wallet | **a minha carteira**
[a 'miɲa kart'ɛjra]

papers | **os meus papéis**
['meuʃ pap'ɛjʃ]

ticket | **o meu bilhete**
[u 'meu biʎ'etɛ]

money | **o dinheiro**
[u diɲ'ɛjru]

handbag | **a minha mala**
[a 'miɲa 'mala]

camera | **a minha câmara**
[a 'miɲa 'kamara]

laptop | **o meu computador**
[u 'meu kõputad'or]

tablet computer | **o meu tablet**
[u 'meu tabl'et]

mobile phone | **o meu telemóvel**
[u 'meu tɛlɛm'ɔvɛl]

Help me! | **Ajude-me!**
[aʒ'udɛmɛ!]

What's happened? | **O que é que aconteceu?**
[u kɛ ɛ kɛ akõtɛs'eu?]

fire | **fogo**
[f'ogu]

shooting	**tiroteio** [tirut'ɛju]
murder	**assassínio** [asas'iniu]
explosion	**explosão** [ɛʃpluz'au]
fight	**briga** [br'iga]

Call the police!	**Chame a polícia!** ['ʃamɛ a pul'isia!]
Please hurry up!	**Mais depressa, por favor!** ['maiʃ dɛpr'ɛsa, pur fav'or!]
I'm looking for the police station.	**Estou à procura de uma esquadra de polícia.** [ʃto a prɔk'ura dɛ 'uma ɛʃku'adra dɛ pul'isia]
I need to make a call.	**Preciso de telefonar.** [prɛs'izu dɛ tɛlɛfun'ar]
May I use your phone?	**Posso telefonar?** ['pɔsu tɛlɛfun'ar?]

I've been …	**Fui …** [fui …]
mugged	**assaltado /assaltada/** [asalt'adu /asalt'ada/]
robbed	**roubado /roubada/** [rob'adu /rob'ada/]
raped	**violada** [viul'ada]
attacked (beaten up)	**atacado /atacada/** [atak'adu /atak'ada/]

Are you all right?	**Está tudo bem consigo?** [ɛʃt'a 'tudu bɛj kõs'igu?]
Did you see who it was?	**Viu quem foi?** ['viu kɛj foj?]
Would you be able to recognize the person?	**Seria capaz de reconhecer a pessoa?** [sɛr'ia kap'aʃ dɛ rɛkuɲɛs'er a pɛs'oa?]
Are you sure?	**Tem a certeza?** [tɛj a sɛrt'eza?]

Please calm down.	**Acalme-se, por favor.** [ak'almɛsɛ, pur fav'or]
Take it easy!	**Calma!** ['kalma!]
Don't worry!	**Não se preocupe.** ['nau sɛ priɔk'upɛ]
Everything will be fine.	**Vai ficar tudo bem.** [vaj fik'ar 'tudu bɛj]
Everything's all right.	**Está tudo em ordem.** [ɛʃt'a 'tudu ɛj 'ɔrdɛj]

Come here, please.	**Chegue aqui, por favor.** ['ʃegɛ ak'ɪ, pur fav'or]
I have some questions for you.	**Tenho algumas questões** **a colocar-lhe.** ['tɛɲu alg'umaʃ kɛʃt'õjʃ a kuluk'arʎɛ]
Wait a moment, please.	**Aguarde um momento, por favor.** [agu'ardɛ ũ mum'ẽtu, pur fav'or]
Do you have any I.D.?	**Tem alguma identificação?** [tɛj alg'uma idẽtifikas'au?]
Thanks. You can leave now.	**Obrigado. Pode ir.** [ɔbrig'adu. 'pɔdɛ ir]
Hands behind your head!	**Mãos atrás da cabeça!** ['mauʃ atr'aʃ da kab'esa!]
You're under arrest!	**Você está preso!** [vɔs'e ɛʃt'a pr'ezu!]

Health problems

Please help me.	**Ajude-me, por favor.** [aʒ'udɛmɛ, pur fav'or]
I don't feel well.	**Não me sinto bem.** ['nau mɛ 'sĩtu bɛj]
My husband doesn't feel well.	**O meu marido não se sente bem.** [u 'meu mar'idu 'nau sɛ 'sẽtɛ bɛj]
My son ...	**O meu filho ...** [u 'meu 'fiʎu ...]
My father ...	**O meu pai ...** [u 'meu 'paj ...]
My wife doesn't feel well.	**A minha mulher não se sente bem.** [a 'miɲa muʎ'ɛr 'nau sɛ 'sẽtɛ bɛj]
My daughter ...	**A minha filha ...** [a 'miɲa 'fiʎa ...]
My mother ...	**A minha mãe ...** [a 'miɲa 'mɛj ...]
I've got a ...	**Tenho uma ...** ['tɛɲu 'uma ...]
headache	**dor de cabeça** [dor dɛ kab'esa]
sore throat	**dor de garganta** [dor dɛ garg'ãta]
stomach ache	**dor de barriga** [dor dɛ bar'iga]
toothache	**dor de dentes** [dor dɛ 'dẽtɛʃ]
I feel dizzy.	**Estou com tonturas.** [ʃto kõ tõt'uraʃ]
He has a fever.	**Ele está com febre.** ['ɛle ɛʃt'a kõ 'fɛbrɛ]
She has a fever.	**Ela está com febre.** ['ɛla ɛʃt'a kõ 'fɛbrɛ]
I can't breathe.	**Não consigo respirar.** ['nau kõs'igu rɛʃpir'ar]
I'm short of breath.	**Estou a sufocar.** [ʃto a sufuk'ar]
I am asthmatic.	**Sou asmático /asmática/.** [so aʒm'atiku /aʒm'atika/]
I am diabetic.	**Sou diabético /diabética/.** [so diab'ɛtiku /diab'ɛtika/]

I can't sleep.	**Estou com insónia.** [ʃto kõ̃ĩs'ɔnia]
food poisoning	**intoxicação alimentar** [itɔksikas'au alimĕt'ar]

It hurts here.	**Dói aqui.** [dɔj ak'i]
Help me!	**Ajude-me!** [aʒ'udɛmɛ!]
I am here!	**Estou aqui!** [ʃto ak'i!]
We are here!	**Estamos aqui!** [ɛʃt'amuʃ ak'i!]
Get me out of here!	**Tirem-me daqui!** ['tirɛjmɛ dak'i!]
I need a doctor.	**Preciso de um médico.** [prɛs'izu dɛ ũ 'mɛdiku]
I can't move.	**Não me consigo mexer.** ['nau mɛ kõs'igu mɛʃ'er]
I can't move my legs.	**Não consigo mover as pernas.** ['nau kõs'igu muv'er aʃ 'pɛrnaʃ]

I have a wound.	**Estou ferido.** [ʃto fɛr'idu]
Is it serious?	**É grave?** [ɛ gr'avɛ?]
My documents are in my pocket.	**Tenho os documentos no bolso.** ['tɛɲu uʃ dukum'ĕtuʃ nu 'bolsu]
Calm down!	**Acalme-se!** [ak'almɛsɛ!]
May I use your phone?	**Posso telefonar?** ['pɔsu tɛlɛfun'ar?]

Call an ambulance!	**Chame a ambulância!** ['ʃamɛ a ãbul'ãsia!]
It's urgent!	**É urgente!** [ɛ urʒ'ĕtɛ!]
It's an emergency!	**É uma emergência!** [ɛ 'uma emɛrʒ'ĕsia!]
Please hurry up!	**Mais depressa, por favor!** ['maiʃ dɛpr'ɛsa, pur fav'or!]
Would you please call a doctor?	**Chame o médico, por favor.** ['ʃamɛ u 'mɛdiku, pur fav'or]
Where is the hospital?	**Onde fica o hospital?** ['õdɛ 'fika u ɔʃpit'al?]

How are you feeling?	**Como se sente?** ['komu sɛ 'sĕtɛ?]
Are you all right?	**Está tudo bem consigo?** [ɛʃt'a 'tudu bɛj kõs'igu?]
What's happened?	**O que é que aconteceu?** [u kɛ ɛ kɛ akõtɛs'eu?]

I feel better now.

Já me sinto melhor.
[ʒa mɛ 'sĩtu mɛʎ'ɔr]

It's OK.

Está tudo em ordem.
[ɛʃt'a 'tudu ɐj 'ɔrdɛj]

It's all right.

Tubo bem.
['tubu bɛj]

At the pharmacy

pharmacy (drugstore)	**farmácia** [farm'asia]
24-hour pharmacy	**farmácia de serviço** [farm'asia dɛ sɛrv'isu]
Where is the closest pharmacy?	**Onde fica a farmácia mais próxima?** ['õdɛ 'fika a farm'asia 'maiʃ pr'ɔsima?]
Is it open now?	**Está aberto agora?** [ɛʃt'a ab'ɛrtu ag'ɔra?]
At what time does it open?	**A que horas abre?** [a kɛ 'ɔraʃ 'abrɛ?]
At what time does it close?	**A que horas fecha?** [a kɛ 'ɔraʃ 'faʃa?]
Is it far?	**Fica longe?** [f'ika 'lõʒɛ?]
Can I get there on foot?	**Posso ir até lá a pé?** ['pɔsu ir atɛ la a pɛ?]
Can you show me on the map?	**Pode-me mostrar no mapa?** ['pɔdɛmɛ muʃtr'ar nu 'mapa?]
Please give me something for ...	**Por favor dê-me algo para ...** [pur fav'or 'dɛmɛ 'algu 'para ...]
a headache	**as dores de cabeça** [aʃ 'dorɛʃ dɛ kab'esa]
a cough	**a tosse** [a 'tɔsɛ]
a cold	**o resfriado** [u ʀeʃfri'adu]
the flu	**a gripe** [a gr'ipɛ]
a fever	**a febre** [a 'fɛbrɛ]
a stomach ache	**uma dor de estômago** ['uma dor dɛ ɛʃt'omagu]
nausea	**as náuseas** [aʃ 'nauziaʃ]
diarrhea	**a diarreia** [a diar'ɛja]
constipation	**a constipação** [a kõʃtipas'au]
pain in the back	**as dores nas costas** [aʃ 'dorɛʃ naʃ 'kɔʃtaʃ]

chest pain	**as dores no peito**
	[aʃ 'dorɛʃ nu 'pɛjtu]
side stitch	**a sutura**
	[a sut'ura]
abdominal pain	**as dores abdominais**
	[aʃ 'dorɛʃ abdumin'ajʃ]

pill	**comprimido**
	[kõprim'idu]
ointment, cream	**unguento, creme**
	[ũgu'ẽtu, kr'ɛmɛ]
syrup	**xarope**
	[ʃar'ɔp]
spray	**spray**
	[spr'aj]
drops	**gotas**
	['gotaʃ]

You need to go to the hospital.	**Você precisa de ir ao hospital.**
	[vɔs'e prɛs'iza dɛ ir 'au ɔʃpit'al]
health insurance	**seguro de saúde**
	[sɛg'uru dɛ sa'udɛ]
prescription	**prescrição**
	[prɛʃkris'au]
insect repellant	**repelente de insetos**
	[rɛpɛl'ẽtɛ dɛ ̄ıs'ɛtuʃ]
Band Aid	**penso rápido**
	['pẽsu 'rapidu]

The bare minimum

Excuse me, ...	**Desculpe, ...** [dɛʃk'ulpɛ, ...]
Hello.	**Olá!** [ɔl'a!]
Thank you.	**Obrigado /Obrigada/.** [ɔbrig'adu /ɔbrig'ada/]
Good bye.	**Adeus.** [ad'euʃ]
Yes.	**Sim.** [sĩ]
No.	**Não.** ['nau]
I don't know.	**Não sei.** ['nau sɛj]
Where? | Where to? | When?	**Onde? | Para onde? | Quando?** ['õdɛ? | 'para 'õdɛ? | ku'ãdu?]
I need ...	**Preciso de ...** [prɛs'izu dɛ ...]
I want ...	**Eu queria ...** ['eu kɛr'ia ...]
Do you have ...?	**Tem ...?** [tɛj ...?]
Is there a ... here?	**Há aqui ...?** ['a ak'i ...?]
May I ...?	**Posso ...?** ['pɔsu ...?]
..., please (polite request)	**..., por favor** [..., pur fav'or]
I'm looking for ...	**Estou à procura de ...** [ʃto a prɔk'ura dɛ ...]
restroom	**casa de banho** ['kaza dɛ 'baɲu]
ATM	**Multibanco** [multib'ãku]
pharmacy (drugstore)	**farmácia** [farm'asia]
hospital	**hospital** [ɔʃpit'al]
police station	**esquadra de polícia** [ɛʃku'adra dɛ pul'isia]
subway	**metro** ['mɛtru]

taxi	**táxi** ['taksi]
train station	**estação de comboio** [ɛʃtas'au dɛ kõb'ɔju]

My name is ...	**Chamo-me ...** ['ʃamumɛ ...]
What's your name?	**Como se chama?** ['komu sɛ ʃ'ama?]
Could you please help me?	**Pode-me dar uma ajuda?** ['pɔdɛmɛ dar 'uma aʒ'uda?]
I've got a problem.	**Tenho um problema.** ['tɛɲu ũ prubl'ema]
I don't feel well.	**Não me sinto bem.** ['nau mɛ 'sĩtu bɛj]
Call an ambulance!	**Chame a ambulância!** ['ʃamɛ a ãbul'ãsia!]
May I make a call?	**Posso fazer uma chamada?** ['pɔsu faz'er 'uma ʃam'ada?]

I'm sorry.	**Desculpe.** [dɛʃk'ulpɛ]
You're welcome.	**De nada.** [dɛ 'nada]

I, me	**eu** ['eu]
you (inform.)	**tu** [tu]
he	**ele** ['ɛlɛ]
she	**ela** ['ɛla]
they (masc.)	**eles** ['ɛleʃ]
they (fem.)	**elas** ['ɛlaʃ]
we	**nós** [nɔʃ]
you (pl)	**vocês** [vɔs'eʃ]
you (sg, form.)	**você** [vɔs'e]

ENTRANCE	**ENTRADA** [ẽtr'ada]
EXIT	**SAÍDA** [sa'ida]
OUT OF ORDER	**FORA DE SERVIÇO** [f'ora dɛ sɛrv'isu]
CLOSED	**FECHADO** [fɛʃ'adu]

OPEN

ABERTO
[ab'ɛrtu]

FOR WOMEN

PARA SENHORAS
['para sɛɲ'oraʃ]

FOR MEN

PARA HOMENS
['para 'ɔmɛjʃ]

MINI DICTIONARY

This section contains 250 useful words required for everyday communication. You will find the names of months and days of the week here. The dictionary also contains topics such as colors, measurements, family, and more

T&P Books Publishing

DICTIONARY CONTENTS

T&P Books Publishing

time	**tempo** (m)	['tẽpu]
hour	**hora** (f)	['ɔɾɐ]
half an hour	**meia hora** (f)	['mɐjɐ 'ɔɾɐ]
minute	**minuto** (m)	[mi'nutu]
second	**segundo** (m)	[sə'gũdu]
today (adv)	**hoje**	['oʒə]
tomorrow (adv)	**amanhã**	[amɐ'ɲã]
yesterday (adv)	**ontem**	['õtẽj]
Monday	**segunda-feira** (f)	[sə'gũdɐ 'fɐjɾɐ]
Tuesday	**terça-feira** (f)	['teɾsɐ 'fɐjɾɐ]
Wednesday	**quarta-feira** (f)	[ku'aɾt 'fɐjɾɐ]
Thursday	**quinta-feira** (f)	['kĩtɐ 'fɐjɾɐ]
Friday	**sexta-feira** (f)	['sɐʃtɐ 'fɐjɾɐ]
Saturday	**sábado** (m)	['sabɐdu]
Sunday	**domingo** (m)	[du'mĩgu]
day	**dia** (m)	['diɐ]
working day	**dia** (m) **de trabalho**	['diɐ də tɾɐ'baʎu]
public holiday	**feriado** (m)	[fɐɾj'adu]
weekend	**fim** (m) **de semana**	[fĩ də sə'mɐnɐ]
week	**semana** (f)	[sə'mɐnɐ]
last week (adv)	**na semana passada**	[nɐ sə'mɐnɐ pɐ'sadɐ]
next week (adv)	**na próxima semana**	[nɐ 'pɾɔsimɐ sə'mɐnɐ]
in the morning	**de manhã**	[də mɐ'ɲã]
in the afternoon	**à tarde**	[a 'taɾdə]
in the evening	**à noite**	[a 'nojtə]
tonight (this evening)	**esta noite, hoje à noite**	['ɛʃtɐ 'nojtə], ['oʒə a 'nojtə]
at night	**à noite**	[a 'nojtə]
midnight	**meia-noite** (f)	['mɐjɐ 'nojtə]
January	**janeiro** (m)	[ʒɐ'nɐjɾu]
February	**fevereiro** (m)	[fɐvə'ɾɐjɾu]
March	**março** (m)	['maɾsu]
April	**abril** (m)	[ɐ'bɾil]
May	**maio** (m)	['maju]
June	**junho** (m)	['ʒuɲu]
July	**julho** (m)	['ʒuʎu]
August	**agosto** (m)	[ɐ'goʃtu]

September	setembro (m)	[sə'tɛ̃bru]
October	outubro (m)	[o'tubru]
November	novembro (m)	[nu'vɛ̃bru]
December	dezembro (m)	[də'zɛ̃bru]

in spring	na primavera	[nɐ primɐ'vɛɾɐ]
in summer	no verão	[nu vɐ'rãu]
in fall	no outono	[nu o'tonu]
in winter	no inverno	[nu ĩ'vɛɾnu]

month	mês (m)	[meʃ]
season (summer, etc.)	estação (f)	[əʃtɐ'sãu]
year	ano (m)	['ɐnu]

2. Numbers. Numerals

0 zero	zero	['zɛɾu]
1 one	um	[ũ]
2 two	dois	[doɪʃ]
3 three	três	[treʃ]
4 four	quatro	[ku'atru]

5 five	cinco	['sĩku]
6 six	seis	['seɪʃ]
7 seven	sete	['sɛtə]
8 eight	oito	['ojtu]
9 nine	nove	['nɔvə]
10 ten	dez	[dɛʒ]

11 eleven	onze	['õzə]
12 twelve	doze	['dozə]
13 thirteen	treze	['trezə]
14 fourteen	catorze	[kɐ'torzə]
15 fifteen	quinze	['kĩzə]

16 sixteen	dezasseis	[dəzɐ'seɪʃ]
17 seventeen	dezassete	[dəzɐ'sɛtə]
18 eighteen	dezoito	[də'zɔjtu]
19 nineteen	dezanove	[dəzɐ'nɔvə]

20 twenty	vinte	['vĩtə]
30 thirty	trinta	['trĩtə]
40 forty	quarenta	[kuɐ'rɛ̃tə]
50 fifty	cinquenta	[sĩku'ɛ̃tə]

60 sixty	sessenta	[sə'sɛ̃tə]
70 seventy	setenta	[sə'tɛ̃tə]
80 eighty	oitenta	[oj'tɛ̃tə]
90 ninety	noventa	[nu'vɛ̃tə]
100 one hundred	cem	[sɛ̃']

200 two hundred	**duzentos**	[du'zẽtuʃ]
300 three hundred	**trezentos**	[trə'zẽtuʃ]
400 four hundred	**quatrocentos**	[kuatru'sẽtuʃ]
500 five hundred	**quinhentos**	[ki'ɲẽtuʃ]
600 six hundred	**seiscentos**	[seɪ'ʃẽtuʃ]
700 seven hundred	**setecentos**	[sɛtə'sẽtuʃ]
800 eight hundred	**oitocentos**	[ojtu'sẽtuʃ]
900 nine hundred	**novecentos**	[nɔvə'sẽtuʃ]
1000 one thousand	**mil**	[mil]
10000 ten thousand	**dez mil**	['dɛʒ mil]
one hundred thousand	**cem mil**	[sẽⁱ mil]
million	**um milhão**	[ũ mi'ʎãu]
billion	**mil milhões**	[mil mi'ʎoɪʃ]

3. Humans. Family

man (adult male)	**homem** (m)	['ɔmẽⁱ]
young man	**jovem** (m)	['ʒɔvẽⁱ]
woman	**mulher** (f)	[mu'ʎɛr]
girl (young woman)	**rapariga** (f)	[ʀɐpɐ'rigɐ]
old man	**velhote** (m)	[vɛ'ʎɔtə]
old woman	**velhota** (f)	[vɛ'ʎɔtɐ]
mother	**mãe** (f)	[mẽⁱ]
father	**pai** (m)	[paj]
son	**filho** (m)	['fiʎu]
daughter	**filha** (f)	['fiʎɐ]
brother	**irmão** (m)	[i'rmãu]
sister	**irmã** (f)	[i'rmã]
parents	**pais** (pl)	['paɪʃ]
child	**criança** (f)	[krj'ãsɐ]
children	**crianças** (f pl)	[krj'ãsɐʃ]
stepmother	**madrasta** (f)	[mɐ'draʃtɐ]
stepfather	**padrasto** (m)	[pɐ'draʃtu]
grandmother	**avó** (f)	[ɐ'vɔ]
grandfather	**avô** (m)	[ɐ'vo]
grandson	**neto** (m)	['nɛtu]
granddaughter	**neta** (f)	['nɛtɐ]
grandchildren	**netos** (pl)	['nɛtuʃ]
uncle	**tio** (m)	['tiu]
aunt	**tia** (f)	['tiɐ]
nephew	**sobrinho** (m)	[su'briɲu]
niece	**sobrinha** (f)	[su'briɲɐ]
wife	**mulher** (f)	[mu'ʎɛr]

husband	marido (m)	[mɐ'ridu]
married (masc.)	casado	[kɐ'zadu]
married (fem.)	casada	[kɐ'zadɐ]
widow	viúva (f)	['vjuvɐ]
widower	viúvo (m)	['vjuvu]

| name (first name) | nome (m) | ['nomə] |
| surname (last name) | apelido (m) | [ɐpə'lidu] |

relative	parente (m)	[pɐ'rẽtə]
friend (masc.)	amigo (m)	[ɐ'migu]
friendship	amizade (f)	[ɐmi'zadə]

partner	parceiro (m)	[pɐ'rsɐjru]
superior (n)	superior (m)	[supərj'or]
colleague	colega (m)	[ku'lɛgɐ]
neighbors	vizinhos (pl)	[vi'ziɲuʃ]

4. Human body

body	corpo (m)	['korpu]
heart	coração (m)	[kurɐ'sãu]
blood	sangue (m)	['sãgə]
brain	cérebro (m)	['sɛrəbru]

bone	osso (m)	['osu]
spine (backbone)	coluna (f) vertebral	[ku'lunɐ vərtə'bral]
rib	costela (f)	[ku'ʃtɛlɐ]
lungs	pulmões (m pl)	[pu'lmoɪʃ]
skin	pele (f)	['pɛlə]

head	cabeça (f)	[kɐ'besɐ]
face	cara (f)	['karɐ]
nose	nariz (m)	[nɐ'riʒ]
forehead	testa (f)	['tɛʃtɐ]
cheek	bochecha (f)	[bu'ʃeʃɐ]

mouth	boca (f)	['bokɐ]
tongue	língua (f)	['lĩguɐ]
tooth	dente (m)	['dẽtə]
lips	lábios (m pl)	['labiuʃ]
chin	queixo (m)	['kɐɪʃu]

ear	orelha (f)	[ɔ'rɐʎɐ]
neck	pescoço (m), colo (m)	[pə'ʃkosu], ['kɔlu]
eye	olho (m)	['oʎu]
pupil	pupila (f)	[pu'pilɐ]
eyebrow	sobrancelha (f)	[subrã'sɐʎɐ]
eyelash	pestana (f)	[pə'ʃtɐnɐ]
hair	cabelos (m pl)	[kɐ'beluʃ]

hairstyle	**penteado** (m)	[pẽtj'adu]
mustache	**bigode** (m)	[bi'gɔdə]
beard	**barba** (f)	['barbə]
to have (a beard, etc.)	**usar, ter** (vt)	[u'zar], [ter]
bald (adj)	**calvo**	['kalvu]
hand	**mão** (f)	['mãu]
arm	**braço** (m)	['brasu]
finger	**dedo** (m)	['dedu]
nail	**unha** (f)	['uɲɐ]
palm	**palma** (f)	['palmɐ]
shoulder	**ombro** (m)	['õbru]
leg	**perna** (f)	['pɛrnɐ]
knee	**joelho** (m)	[ʒu'ɐʎu]
heel	**talão** (m)	[tɐ'lẽw̃]
back	**costas** (f pl)	['kɔʃtɐʃ]

5. Clothing. Personal accessories

clothes	**roupa** (f)	['ʀopɐ]
coat (overcoat)	**sobretudo** (m)	[sobrɐ'tudu]
fur coat	**casaco** (m) **de peles**	[kɐ'zaku də 'pɛləʃ]
jacket (e.g., leather ~)	**casaco, blusão** (m)	[kɐ'zaku], [blu'zãu]
raincoat (trenchcoat, etc.)	**impermeável** (m)	[ipərmi'avɛl]
shirt (button shirt)	**camisa** (f)	[kɐ'mizɐ]
pants	**calças** (f pl)	['kalsɐʃ]
suit jacket	**casaco** (m)	[kɐ'zaku]
suit	**fato** (m)	['fatu]
dress (frock)	**vestido** (m)	[vɐ'ʃtidu]
skirt	**saia** (f)	['sajɐ]
T-shirt	**T-shirt, camiseta** (f)	['tiʃərt], [kɐmi'zetɐ]
bathrobe	**roupão** (m) **de banho**	[ʀo'pãu də 'bɐɲu]
pajamas	**pijama** (m)	[pi'ʒɐmɐ]
workwear	**roupa** (f) **de trabalho**	['ʀopɐ də trɐ'baʎu]
underwear	**roupa** (f) **interior**	['ʀopɐ ĩtərj'or]
socks	**peúgas** (f pl)	[pj'ugɐʃ]
bra	**sutiã** (m)	[sutj'ã]
pantyhose	**meias-calças** (f pl)	['mɐjɐʃ 'kalsɐʃ]
stockings (thigh highs)	**meias** (f pl)	['mɐjɐʃ]
bathing suit	**fato** (m) **de banho**	['fatu də 'bɐɲu]
hat	**chapéu** (m)	[ʃɐ'pɛu]
footwear	**calçado** (m)	[ka'lsadu]
boots (cowboy ~)	**botas** (f pl)	['botɐʃ]
heel	**salto** (m)	['saltu]
shoestring	**atacador** (m)	[ɐtɐkɐ'dor]

shoe polish	**graxa** (f) **para calçado**	['graʃɐ 'peɾɐ ka'lsadu]
gloves	**luvas** (f pl)	['luveʃ]
mittens	**mitenes** (f pl)	[mi'tɛnɐʃ]
scarf (muffler)	**cachecol** (m)	[kaʃɐ'kɔl]
glasses (eyeglasses)	**óculos** (m pl)	['ɔkuluʃ]
umbrella	**guarda-chuva** (m)	[guɐɾdɐ 'ʃuvɐ]
tie (necktie)	**gravata** (f)	[gɾɐ'vatɐ]
handkerchief	**lenço** (m)	['lẽsu]
comb	**pente** (m)	['pẽtɐ]
hairbrush	**escova** (f) **para o cabelo**	[ə'ʃkovɐ 'peɾɐ u kɐ'belu]
buckle	**fivela** (f)	[fi'vɛlɐ]
belt	**cinto** (m)	['sĩtu]
purse	**bolsa** (f) **de senhora**	['bolsɐ dɐ sɐ'ɲoɾɐ]

6. House. Apartment

apartment	**apartamento** (m)	[ɐpɐɾtɐ'mẽtu]
room	**quarto** (m)	[ku'aɾtu]
bedroom	**quarto** (m) **de dormir**	[ku'aɾtu dɐ du'ɾmiɾ]
dining room	**sala** (f) **de jantar**	['salɐ dɐ ʒã'taɾ]
living room	**sala** (f) **de estar**	['salɐ dɐ ə'ʃtaɾ]
study (home office)	**escritório** (m)	[əʃkɾi'tɔɾiu]
entry room	**antessala** (f)	[ãtə'salɐ]
bathroom (room with a bath or shower)	**quarto** (m) **de banho**	[ku'aɾtu dɐ 'beɲu]
half bath	**quarto** (m) **de banho**	[ku'aɾtu dɐ 'beɲu]
vacuum cleaner	**aspirador** (m)	[əʃpiɾɐ'doɾ]
mop	**esfregona** (f)	[əʃfrɐ'gonɐ]
dust cloth	**pano** (m), **trapo** (m)	['penu], ['tɾapu]
short broom	**vassoura** (f)	[vɐ'soɾɐ]
dustpan	**pá** (f) **de lixo**	[pa dɐ 'liʃu]
furniture	**mobiliário** (m)	[mubilj'aɾiu]
table	**mesa** (f)	['mezɐ]
chair	**cadeira** (f)	[kɐ'dejɾɐ]
armchair	**cadeirão** (m)	[kɐdej'rãu]
mirror	**espelho** (m)	[ə'ʃpeʎu]
carpet	**tapete** (m)	[tɐ'petɐ]
fireplace	**lareira** (f)	[lɐ'rejɾɐ]
drapes	**cortinas** (f pl)	[ku'ɾtinɐʃ]
table lamp	**candeeiro** (m) **de mesa**	[kãdj'ejɾu dɐ 'mezɐ]
chandelier	**lustre** (m)	['luʃtɾɐ]
kitchen	**cozinha** (f)	[ku'ziɲɐ]
gas stove (range)	**fogão** (m) **a gás**	[fu'gãu ɐ gaʃ]

electric stove	**fogão** (m) **elétrico**	[fuˈgãu eˈlɛtriku]
microwave oven	**forno** (m) **de micro-ondas**	[ˈfornu də mikrɔˈõdəʃ]
refrigerator	**frigorífico** (m)	[friguˈrifiku]
freezer	**congelador** (m)	[kõʒələˈdor]
dishwasher	**máquina** (f) **de lavar louça**	[ˈmakinɐ də lɐˈvar ˈlosɐ]
faucet	**torneira** (f)	[tuˈrnejrɐ]
meat grinder	**moedor** (m) **de carne**	[muɐˈdor də ˈkarnə]
juicer	**espremedor** (m)	[əʃprəməˈdor]
toaster	**torradeira** (f)	[tuʀɐˈdejɾɐ]
mixer	**batedeira** (f)	[bɐtɐˈdejɾɐ]
coffee machine	**máquina** (f) **de café**	[ˈmakinɐ də kɐˈfɛ]
kettle	**chaleira** (f)	[ʃɐˈlejɾɐ]
teapot	**bule** (m)	[ˈbulə]
TV set	**televisor** (m)	[tələviˈzor]
VCR (video recorder)	**videogravador** (m)	[vidiɔgrɐvɐˈdor]
iron (e.g., steam ~)	**ferro** (m) **de engomar**	[ˈfɛʀu də ẽguˈmar]
telephone	**telefone** (m)	[tələˈfonə]

www.ingramcontent.com/pod-product-compliance
Lightning Source LLC
Chambersburg PA
CBHW071505070426
42452CB00041B/2304